Guitar for Beginners, Volume 1

Easy Acoustic Guitar Lessons for Complete Beginners

by James Shipway

Guitar for Beginners, Volume 1
by James Shipway

Published by Headstock Books
headstockbooks.com

Paperback ISBN: 978-1-914453-93-9
Hardcover ISBN: 978-1-914453-80-9 / 978-1-914453-81-6
Spiralbound ISBN: 978-1-914453-72-4
Ebook ISBN: 978-1-914453-94-6

Search for 'james shipway guitar' on YouTube and
subscribe for hours of free video lessons!

Join my online community at **totalguitarlab.com** and
get instant access to *all* my premium guitar courses *plus* live training,
workshops and Q&A sessions.

Contents

Grab Your Free Workbook and Play–along Tracks Before You Start!

Before you get started, make sure to download the **free printable workbook** and **backing tracks** which accompany this book. Inside the **workbook** you'll find:

- **Song sheets** for all the songs we're going to play in this method book. You can print these and put them on your music stand which you might find easier than reading them from this book
- **Chord shape** wall chart/sheet
- **Checklists** for each chapter - use these to track your progress

The **play-along backing tracks** are a *perfect* way for you to practice the songs in this book. Using these will help you gain confidence and improve faster.

I suggest you grab these valuable bonus resources before you start, simply go to the address below and follow the instructions on the page:

start-guitar.com

Important: <u>This Book Also Comes with a Website!</u>

I've created an accompanying website for this book series where you can watch videos demonstrating the important concepts, exercises and the songs we'll be playing. This means you get to hear and see how things are supposed to sound. Video content includes:

- **Play-along video demos** of all the songs we'll use in this book series
- **Demo videos** of most of the **chords** and **strumming patterns** we're going to cover
- Lessons on **tuning your guitar**, **strumming techniques**, **learning chord shapes** and much more

The website is completely free to access and will make a big difference to how successfully you are able to use this book, so be sure to make the most of this valuable bonus content. Check it out at the following web address: **start-guitar.com**

Note: Remember to include the hyphen when you type the web address in to your browser

Introduction

Hello and welcome to **Guitar for Beginners, Volume 1**. This is the first book in my *Guitar for Beginners* series and it's great to have you here!

You likely picked up this book for one of the following reasons:

- You've always wanted to play the guitar but don't know how to start
- You've tried learning guitar before but found it confusing, difficult or impossible
- You want to play songs you love on the guitar but have no clue how to
- You play a bit already but are frustrated by your limitations and lack of progress
- You're a singer/songwriter and want to develop basic guitar skills to accompany yourself
- You want to understand the basics in order to enjoy making music with others - whether at parties, open mic nights, in a band, a worship group or another setting

Whatever your personal motivation, if you're looking for a straightforward, easy-to-use method for learning to play the guitar, you're in the right place.

Before we start, there are some important things we need to clear up - these will help you find success with this book and others in the *Guitar for Beginners* series.

Can *everyone* learn to play the guitar?

When I first picked up the guitar I was a bit afraid. I'd never successfully played an instrument before and didn't think of myself as being very musical.

So, whilst I dreamed of being able to play the guitar, I was scared that I might not have what it took and would be forced to admit that I was a musical failure!

Years later, I've made a *career* from playing, teaching and writing about the guitar. I've figured out and learned hundreds (if not *thousands*) of songs, composed and recorded my own music, worked with bands, in studios, and much more. My self-judgement about not being musical was nonsense, a story I told myself which was based on absolutely no evidence whatsoever.

I've heard *hundreds* of beginner guitar students repeat the things I told myself, things like:

- I'm not musical
- I've got no sense of rhythm
- I'm tone deaf and can't sing in tune

When I ask them *why* they've formed these opinions of themselves, they don't normally know and there's really no evidence for what they're saying. And guess what? In most cases, they're surprised by what they can do after just a short time, and they end up getting immense pleasure from playing the guitar.

I tell you this because I *know* that there are people reading this book who have similar thoughts about themselves and their musical potential. I'm here to say that these stories are probably *not* true.

Some readers will be thinking:

- It's going to be hard for me because my hands are small
- I'm too old to learn the guitar!
- I tried learning guitar before and gave up
- I can't read music

None of these things really matter either. I've successfully taught many people with small hands, total beginners in their eighties, and lots of people who had made several attempts to learn in the past. Oh, and being able to read music can sometimes be helpful, but certainly isn't necessary (it's true).

After around *30,000* hours spent teaching guitar, I've made a lot of discoveries, and one of them is that *almost anyone* can learn to play and enjoy the guitar. Like any skill, some people take to it more naturally and learn faster than others, but with a bit of dedication and perseverance, I'm pretty confident that you will soon be enjoying playing the guitar.

So leave any stories and pre-conceptions behind as you start this book, you don't need them holding you back. Begin your guitar journey feeling confident, positive and excited. You're about to learn a cool new skill – just focus on moving forward with it.

Why another beginner book series?

There are *hundreds* of beginner books out there already, but many of them don't seem to work. Browse reader reviews and you start to feel that many are not written with the beginner in mind - they're often confusing, and important points are not well explained. What's more, they don't address the common roadblocks *all* beginners face nor show how to overcome them. The authors may be able to play the guitar, but I'm often left wondering if they've ever taught *somebody else* how to play!

As I said earlier, I've spent over 30,000 hours teaching guitar, a huge chunk of these hours have been spent teaching *complete* beginners. I've seen *up-close* what most people struggle with, what confuses them, and what holds them up and I've had to develop methods for teaching beginners which actually *work*.

That's why this book is different from many others. You see, you're not just getting a load of beginner guitar information, you're getting my **proven method** for learning guitar. My way is not the *only* way to learn guitar, but it has worked for hundreds and hundreds of guitar players already, and if you apply yourself, I'm pretty sure it will work for you too. All you need to do is follow the steps I set out for you.

What this book will do for you?

This is Volume 1 in my *Guitar for Beginners* series. It assumes no prior knowledge and is suitable for *total* beginners.

The aim of my *Guitar for Beginners* series is to teach you what you need to become confident playing most pop/rock/country/folk songs on the guitar. Being able to do this is probably *why* you want to play - most people aren't drawn to the guitar because they want to play exercises and scales, they want to be able to bash out songs they like and which people will recognise ...and sound halfway decent doing it!

The goal of this book is to get you on the way to attaining this goal, and to do it with a ***minimum*** amount of knowledge. Many beginner books will show you more *information* than you'll find in this book, but my aim is not to overwhelm you with things you don't need to know, rather to get you up and running playing *music* as quickly as possible.

To be clear, this book is the first in a series, it's not a complete method and will only take you so far. I think you'll probably be amazed by what the simple steps in this book enable you to do, and you'll want to add to your knowledge and skills by continuing with books 2 and 3. Taken together, the 3 books in the *Guitar for Beginners* series provide what I consider to be a complete method for taking your playing to a certain level.

So what are we going to cover in Volume 1? Well, we're going to look at:

- understanding the guitar and how it works
- tuning your guitar with a tuner
- chord shapes

- how to strum and strumming patterns
- learning to change between chords
- reading basic song sheets and playing simple songs
- very basic music theory concepts

...and much more!

It may seem unbelievable right now, but even with just this basic knowledge you can play literally *thousands* of well-known songs. This is one of the reasons the guitar is such a popular instrument; with just a *little* knowledge you can play a *lot* of music!

About the Lessons in this Book

This book features 12 bite-sized lessons designed to teach you one or more specific topics, without overloading you with information.

The lessons use a mixture of:

- **Text/explanations** teaching you core concepts and knowledge
- **Practical Exercises** for building specific guitar skills
- **Pro Tips** giving you 'insider knowledge' so that you can avoid common mistakes and make super-fast progress!
- **Quickfire Lessons** and **Quick Theory Lessons** to develop your understanding of music as you build your playing skills
- **Quiz Questions** for testing your knowledge of certain topics

Many things are easier to learn if you can *see* them being demonstrated and *listen* to how they sound. For this reason, I've supplemented this book with **video lessons** and **demonstrations** and I'll direct you towards them when necessary. Videos are on the **website** that accompanies this book series at:

start-guitar.com

I'm confident that by using these different teaching methods you'll find it easier to remember things, you'll improve quicker, and you'll enjoy the process of learning to play the guitar more.

About the Songs in this Series

The songs in this book series are based on some of the most popular guitar songs suited to beginners.

Unfortunately due to copyright and intellectual property laws, I can't teach you other people's exact songs. Instead, I'm giving you sound-alike versions. When learning a song, visit **start-guitar.com** to see which famous song it is based on - this will really help your performance.

I've chosen songs which I have taught to my guitar students and which I think you will benefit from learning. I appreciate that my choice of songs won't be to every reader's taste, but the skills they'll teach you are directly transferable to *other* songs. In other words, learning the songs in this series will enable you to play *hundreds* of other similar songs as well - including (hopefully) your personal favourites!

In all cases I've simplified, shortened, and sometimes changed the key (don't worry if you don't know what this means) in my version compared to the original song. This is so that the songs are more playable and work better within the context of this method. But don't worry, by using this series, you'll eventually have the skills needed to learn the original songs my simplified versions are based on if you want to.

Don't forget to watch the **demo video** for each song to hear how they should sound when performed. When you feel ready you can play along with the **demo video** or the **backing track** for the song.

You'll find a **printable version** of all the songs in the free **workbook** which accompanies this method, print these off and place them on your music stand when you practice. This may be easier than using the song sheets shown in this book. See the very start of this book to find out how to download your workbook and backing tracks.

How Songs and Examples are Written in this Book

In case you're wondering:

You do not need to be able to read music to use this book!

I will be using some *very basic* musical notation when writing out songs and examples for you, but don't worry, everything will be clearly explained and made easy to understand. This will help you quickly get used to the standard way songs are usually written out for guitar.

I believe this knowledge will be very valuable, making it possible for you to learn from many *other* resources besides just this book series.

Hang on a minute! Don't you <u>have</u> to be able to read music to learn an instrument?

Not with the guitar, in fact you can easily learn what you need to know using other methods, most of which work better anyway. Reading music is a skill you can learn some other time if you need to, we won't be focusing on it in this book series. If you already read music then you may find it helpful in places, but it's certainly not required.

What To Do If You're Left Handed

Most books (including this one) talk about guitar playing from the perspective of a right-handed guitar player. In other words, the left hand is on the guitar neck and the right hand strikes the strings to create a sound. When playing left-handed these roles are reversed.

Whether you're naturally left or right handed makes no difference when it comes to becoming awesome on the guitar, but learning to play left-handed does present some challenges when using most resources (including this book). I've taught *dozens* of left-handed people to play the guitar *right-handed*, and in my opinion this is often the best option for left-handers.

If you disagree, and want to learn to play left-handed then go ahead - but **make sure to read Appendix 1 at the back of this book because there are some super-important things to be aware of**!

How Should You Use This Book?

Before we begin, here are some super-important tips to help you get maximum benefit from this book.

1. Start at the beginning and go through the lessons in the order they are presented

I've chosen to cover the absolute basics at the start of this book because I've found *not* understanding them is what holds *most* players up later on. I want to make sure that this doesn't happen to you. If you find some of the introductory material obvious, or think you know it already - read it anyway. It will be good for revision purposes and will ensure you really do understand the important basics.

2. Test yourself with the quiz questions!

Throughout the book you'll find quiz questions. Use these to check your understanding - this is a quick way to make sure you've really grasped a topic.

3. Go at your own pace

How quickly you work through this book will depend on a number of different factors. Go at a pace which suits **you** and resist the natural instinct most of us have to rush! In my experience, rushing results in slower progress - so take your time.

4. Spend long enough on each lesson

Spend long enough on a lesson to allow the practical skills and knowledge it teaches you to sink in and develop. How long this takes will be different for each reader, so you need to decide when you're ready to move on to the next lesson. It's important to be *honest* with yourself when making this assessment.

I've done my best to make everything easy to understand, but you should read the material in each lesson *multiple* times to help you to retain it.

5. Keep your guitar in sight!

If your guitar is hidden away you're *far* less likely to pick it up and practice. I know this from my own experience. Get a guitar stand or wall hanger, and keep your guitar where you'll see it. This will remind you to play it.

6. Persist and be patient

Be patient, you're learning a new skill, something you'll be able to enjoy for the rest of your life! Don't be disappointed if you don't see *amazing* results overnight. We all improve and progress at different rates, the important thing is to methodically work through this book and not give up. Do this, and you'll be unstoppable in your quest to become a guitar player.

When you get stuck, don't worry, it's not just you - *all* players experience problems, even guitarists who have been playing for years. Just keep going.

There's absolutely nothing wrong with asking for help either. If you've got friends who play guitar, ask them about their experiences learning, they may be able to pass on some useful tips, perhaps some I don't know about! You can also get useful advice from websites like YouTube, other guitar books, plus of course, one-on-one guitar lessons. Beware of overloading yourself with *too much* information though, it can easily pull you off-track, something that happens to many players. You don't need to know *all* the possible ways to play something - especially when you're getting started.

If you follow all these tips, they'll help you get great results and make your learning more enjoyable.

Now it's time to jump into our first chapter where we're going to study some important guitar knowledge you need to get off to a flying-start. See you there!

Chapter 1 – First Steps (Lessons 1–4)

By the end of this chapter you'll have the knowledge you need to successfully start learning the guitar. The material in this chapter may seem very basic, but it's super important, so make sure to study it properly. Working through these first four lessons shouldn't take you too long, but take your time and allow all the important information covered to thoroughly sink in.

I hope you're excited to get started - let's begin.

Lesson 1 - Getting To Know the Guitar

Let's start right at the beginning by learning some of the essential knowledge you need to get started. Without this information, most of the other lessons won't make much sense! We're going to cover:

- Basic parts of the guitar
- The names of the guitar strings
- Frets: what they are and why they're so important
- Other must-know concepts you need to understand

The Parts of the Guitar

I'm mainly concerned with showing you what you need in order to start *playing*, not in covering the structure of the guitar in detail just for the sake of it. The following image shows you the basic parts of the guitar.

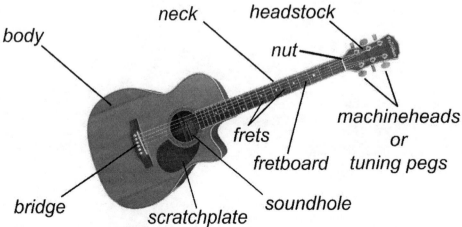

This information is important because I'll use it to describe certain actions.

For example I might say: *'Strum over the **soundhole'**, or 'press the strings into the **fretboard'**, and* if you understand the basic structure of the guitar, then instructions like these will make sense. Take a few minutes to study the diagram, then try the following exercise.

Exercise: Find the Guitar Parts

Identify the following parts of your guitar. Then check your answers using the diagram you saw a moment ago.

1) Headstock
2) Bridge
3) Body
4) Nut

5) Machine head/tuning peg
6) Neck
7) Frets
8) Fretboard

Learning the Guitar Strings

A standard acoustic or electric guitar has **6 strings**, and each one has a name. Properly learning the string names is something many players skip over, but it's absolutely *essential*.

Start on the **thickest** string on the guitar. This is called the low or bottom **E** string. Starting there and going across the strings in order we get the **A**, **D**, **G**, **B** strings. The **thinnest** string is called the top or high **E** string. This is illustrated in these next diagrams.

Take a minute to memorise the order of the strings starting from the thickest string - it's **E, A, D, G, B** and **E.** There's a handy phrase to help you remember the string names. It may be a strange phrase, but it works!

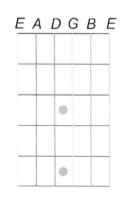

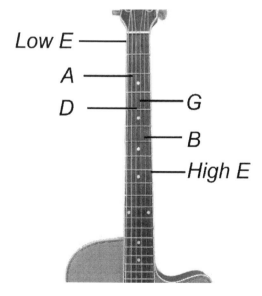

Eddie **A**te **D**ynamite
Good **B**ye **E**ddie

Take the first letter from each word and you get **E, A, D, G, B** and **E** - the names of the guitar strings. Use this to help you, just remember the rhyme starts on the **low E** (thickest string)!

Exercise: String Names

Every time you sit down to practice, spend a few minutes memorising the names of the strings. Do this until you know them *perfectly - not* knowing this information will really slow you down.

When you think you've mastered string names, test yourself using the **String Naming Exercise video** which you'll find in the **Volume 1 videos** section at **start-guitar.com**

Quickfire Lesson: Where Do These String Names Come From?

Strings are named according to the **notes** they are normally tuned to. For example, the G string is tuned to the note G. This means that if you played the G key on a piano and the G string on the guitar they would sound the same (assuming the two were in tune with each other). In the same way, the D string is tuned to the note D.

This explains why the strings are named the way they are. And don't worry, we'll be looking at musical **notes** in the next lesson if you're not sure what they are.

Sometimes you may hear people label the strings with numbers, for example 'the second string' or the 'sixth string'. All you need to remember is that the **thinnest** string (the top E) is the *first* string and the numbers then go across the strings in order. The numbering is therefore:

  1 - **E** (high/top E) - *the first string*
  2 - **B** - *the second string*
  3 - **G** - *the third string*
  4 - **D** - *the fourth string*
  5 - **A** - *the fifth string*
  6 - **E** (low/bottom E) - *the sixth string*

Fret Numbering and 'Open Strings'

The **frets** are the **metal strips** dividing up the fingerboard of the guitar. A sound is produced by pressing down a string in the space between any two frets (called *fretting*) and striking it. It's the gaps *between* the frets that we use, we never normally press a string down on the fret itself.

These gaps are numbered starting from the fret nearest the headstock. This is shown in the following diagram. Only frets 1-12 are numbered, but the numbering keeps going until you run out of frets. The string names are shown on the left of the diagram (the low E string is shown at the bottom).

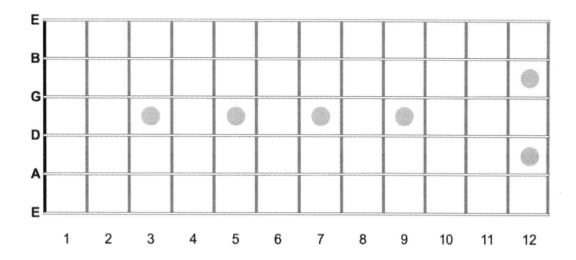

Many guitars have **fret markers** (usually circles) set into the fingerboard and/or along the top edge of the neck. These are normally found at the 3rd, 5th, 7th, 9th and 12th frets (plus some higher frets) and make it easier for guitarists to navigate around the neck. You can see these on the diagram above, shown as grey circles.

When we play a string *without* fretting it (i.e. without simultaneously pressing it down on the fretboard) we're playing an **open string**. Open strings are played a lot, especially when you're starting out, so be prepared to see them again very soon.

Quick Quiz

1) Where is the 3rd fret on your guitar?
2) Where is the 5th fret?
3) Find the 2nd fret on your guitar
4) What is meant by an open string?

If you're not sure of some of these things, see the explanations from a moment ago!

That's all for Lesson 1: Ready To Move On?

Now you know some of the guitar basics you'll need in order to start playing. Let's find out if you're ready for the next lesson:

- Can you identify the main parts of the guitar?
- Can you easily and quickly name any of the guitar strings?
- Do you understand frets, fret numbers and open strings?

If the answer to some of these questions is 'no', don't worry, just spend a bit more time on this lesson. When you can honestly answer 'yes' to all of them, move on to Lesson 2!

Lesson 2 - Music Basics and Your First Chord

In Lesson 2 we're going to look at some more of the beginner essentials you need to know. We're going to cover:

- Notes and chords: what are they?
- Chord shapes: what they are and how do we use them?
- How to play the E minor chord shape
- What do we mean by 'major' and 'minor'?

Let's get started.

Quick Theory Lesson: Notes and Chords

Welcome to the first *Quick Theory Lesson*! These short lessons aim to give you a basic understanding of some useful music theory topics. When I say 'basic', that's exactly what I mean: these lessons are not designed to give you the *complete* picture, just help you as you work through this book series.

What is a *note*?

A **note** is what we call a **single sound**. On an instrument like a piano we get a single note by pressing down one key on its own. On the guitar, a single note is created by plucking a single string.

Grab your guitar and pluck a single open string on its own. Next, press down any string in between any two frets on the fingerboard and pluck it. In both cases you're playing a note - a **single sound**.

There are only 12 notes used in any of the music you're likely to ever play. These 12 notes are combined in all sorts of ways to create music, similar to how we combine the letters in the alphabet to create words and sentences. Just think - all the music that has ever been created has only ever used the same 12 notes, just in different combinations - amazing!

Hang on! The guitar only has 6 strings, how can we possibly play 12 notes?

By pressing down the strings at the different frets on the fingerboard, we are able to play *all* the possible notes. The note we're playing is determined by *which string* we play and *where we press it down* (fret it) on the neck.

What is a *chord*?

A **chord** is several notes played together. On the guitar, we get a chord by pressing down and striking multiple strings together. To start with, you'll be playing chords which use a *mixture* of fretted and open strings.

For convenience, we play chords on the guitar using **chord shapes**. These are simply shapes which we make on the guitar fretboard with our fingers. These make getting started on the guitar pretty easy - with just a few chord shapes, you can start strumming and playing chords. To begin with, you don't even need to know what the notes in the chord are, simply playing the shape is all that is required.

Quick Quiz

1) What is a **note**?
2) What is a **chord**?

Check your answers using the information you've been given on this topic!

The E minor Chord Shape

Let's learn how to play the E minor chord shape (written Em). This is an easy chord shape to start off with, it's also very common and used in lots of songs. To play **Em**:

- Press down the **A string** in the **2nd fret**. Use the **1st finger** (index finger) on your fretting hand
- Press down the **D string** in the **2nd fret**. Use the **2nd finger** (middle finger) on your fretting hand
- Holding these strings down, strum all the strings on your guitar

Congratulations, you just played an Em (E minor) chord shape. You can see this chord shape demonstrated in the **Chord Shape videos** section at **start-guitar.com**

The Em chord written out as a chord diagram is shown in the following image. You may like to try and decipher this once you know the chord shape. If not, it's ok, we'll be looking at reading chord diagrams in Lesson 4.

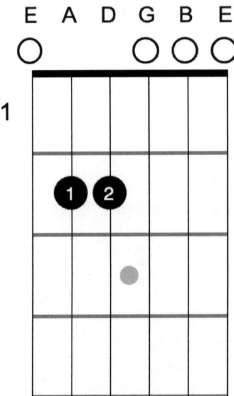

Note: if you're learning to play **left-handed** this chord diagram might be confusing to you, so see Appendix 1 for help!

What do I use chord shapes like this one for?

Chords are normally played to create a **backing** for something. For example, you might play the chords to a song and sing the words over the top.

A song almost never uses a single chord, instead it will use a series of chords played one after the other. This is called a **chord progression** or **chord sequence**. Watch a guitarist play and you'll normally see them changing between different chord shapes with their fretting hand - they're playing a chord progression.

Learning to play songs and chord progressions is a great way to start making music on the guitar, which is why we'll be focusing on learning chord shapes and how to easily switch between them. This might not sound like much, but you'll be amazed what it enables you to do!

Quick Theory Lesson: Major and Minor

There are two main types of chord: **major** and **minor**, each having a different sound. Normally (though not always) chord progressions use a mixture of major and minor chords. Very simply put:

- **Major** chords have a happy, positive, upbeat sound
- **Minor** chords have a sadder, darker sound

When we talk about minor chords we use the full chord name. For example: *'The song starts on **E minor'***

With major chords it's a bit different. We often omit the 'major' part of the chord name, so a G major chord would often just be called 'G'. So, even though we could say: *'The song starts on **C major'**,* we'd likely just say: *'The song starts on **C'.***

So remember, if you ever hear a chord described with *only* a letter name (e.g. F, A, C), then it's a major chord (not a minor chord). You'll get used to this as you work through the lessons in this book.

Quick Quiz

We'll wrap up this lesson with a quiz on some of the things we've covered. Check your answers against those given:

1) What is a note?
2) How many notes are there?
3) What is a chord?
4) What's an easy way to play a chord on the guitar?
5) What is a sequence of chords called?
6) What are the two main types of chord?
7) True or false: An **F major** chord is often simply called **F**?

Answers

1) A note is a **single sound**, for example, plucking one string on the guitar. 2) There are basically **12** possible notes in music. 3) A chord is a **group of notes** played together. 4) Using a **chord shape** is an easy way to learn, play and remember a chord. 5) A sequence of chords is called a **chord progression** or **chord sequence**. 6) The two main types of chord are **major and minor**. 7) **True**. In many cases we miss off the 'major' part of the name when we talk about major chords, labelling them with just their letter name.

That's all for Lesson 2: Ready To Move On?

Now you understand some of the basics you'll need in order to start playing, let's check if you're ready for the next lesson:

- Do you understand what notes and chords are?
- Can you play the Em chord shape?
- Do you know what a chord shape and a chord progression are?
- Do you have a simple understanding of the terms 'major' and 'minor'?

If not, spend a little longer on this lesson. But if you're ready, let's move on to Lesson 3.

Lesson 3 - More Guitar Playing Essentials

This lesson will teach you more of the must-know information you'll need to get off to a flying start on guitar. We'll cover:

- The easiest and quickest way to learn to tune your guitar
- How should you sit and stand when playing?
- How to build a rough practice action-plan
- Fretting hand finger numbers - what do they tell you?

Again, the material in this lesson may not be the most interesting thing about playing the guitar, but it will make a real difference to how well you progress through the rest of this book!

Quickfire Lesson: Sitting and Standing Playing Position

I often get asked if there is a correct way to sit when playing the guitar. I think that for most players, the following guidelines are more than enough when it comes to this topic:

- **Do** sit in a relaxed and comfortable position
- **Do** try not to slump, hunch your shoulders or round your back
- **Don't** force yourself into a position which feels unnatural or uncomfortable
- **Do** experiment to find the best combination of furniture and sitting position for you

I like to sit on a chair which is low enough for me to have my feet on the ground. The guitar can then rest on the top of my right leg. There are alternatives to this, but for most players something similar will work fine.

To play standing up you'll need to fit a guitar strap to your guitar. Relaxation and comfort are important when standing too, and how high you wear the guitar has a big bearing on this. It may look cool to have the guitar slung down around your knees, but it's much harder to play! I like to have the guitar at a similar height to where it is when I sit to play. Experiment and find what's comfortable for you.

So, should you sit or stand when you play? I've found most players find it easiest to sit, but do whatever feels best to you. It's good to eventually become comfortable doing both.

Finger Numbers

The fingers on our fretting hand are numbered for reference purposes. This makes it easy to describe which finger(s) to use to play something on the guitar. The numbers used are as follows:

- **1st** finger - your index/pointing finger
- **2nd** finger - your middle finger
- **3rd** finger - your ring finger
- **4th** finger - your little/pinky finger

We'll be seeing these numbers combined with things like chord diagrams to tell you which fingers to use.

Most players play the guitar right-handed, fretting the strings with the left hand and strumming the strings with the right hand, so for most readers these numbers will apply to the left hand. If you play the guitar left-handed then these numbers will apply to your *right* hand. If you're playing left handed don't forget to check out **Appendix 1** at the back of this book - it's packed full of important info which you need to know.

Video Lesson: Tuning Your Guitar!

No matter how well you play, if your guitar is horribly out of tune - you're in trouble! Being able to tune your guitar is obviously very important. The most reliable way to tune is with an **electronic tuner** or **app**, and fortunately there are lots of great options out there (many of them free).

Describing how to use a tuner would take pages and pages, and it's best to be shown how to do it. For this reason we'll use a video tutorial for this. To learn how to tune your guitar with a tuner watch the **Tuning Your Guitar video** at **start-guitar.com**. You'll find it in the **Volume 1 videos** section.

This will quickly show you the basics of getting your guitar in tune.

Practice Tips

Effective practice habits result in better progress and a more enjoyable guitar journey. Hopefully you're already devoting some time most days to practice what you've been learning in this chapter, but I just want to pass on some advice on this important topic.

1) Aim to make guitar practice a **habit**. Picking up your guitar each day, even if it's only for 10-15 minutes is much better than skipping a practice session, helping build your practice habit
2) Frequent short practice sessions are better than longer, infrequent sessions. Regular repetition (daily when possible) is what really pays off over time. In other words, 10 minutes every day is better than 3 hours on a Sunday!
3) Be realistic about how much practice time you can commit to. Don't over-commit, it normally leads to frustration and feeling demotivated
4) At first, the tips of your fingers will become sore, but after a few weeks they'll toughen up and this won't be a problem. **Salt water** dabbed on the fingertips and left overnight can help the skin to toughen up

Throughout this book we'll be seeing all sorts of practice techniques and exercises to enable you to practice in an efficient and effective way. In the meantime, consider how these points can help you build your practice habit:

1) How much time can you realistically devote each day to learning the guitar? Remember, it doesn't need to be a lot
2) Can you devise a basic schedule/plan outlining *when* you're going to practice? Keep it simple, for example: *Every night before bed/straight after dinner/as soon as I get home from work* - whatever will work for **you**!
3) Why not write your plan somewhere where you'll see it? It'll remind you to make it happen

Having a rough action plan or timetable can make it easier to build a habit and stick at something - so consider drafting one out. Of course, your action plan can be modified and updated whenever you like - you're in charge!

That's all for Lesson 3: Ready To Move On?

OK, now you know some more of the guitar basics you'll need to start playing. Let's find out if you're ready for the next lesson:

- Have you got an electronic tuner/app?
- Can you tune your guitar with it?
- Do you understand how the fretting hand fingers are numbered?
- Have you got a basic action-plan about how and when you're going to practice?

When you can honestly answer 'yes' to all of these questions you're ready to move on to Lesson 4. See you there!

Lesson 4 - Reading Chord Boxes

In this lesson we're going to look at:

- How to read and understand chord boxes

Most of this book involves using chord shapes, so we need to make sure chord diagrams don't confuse you before we go any further.

Note: if you're learning guitar **left-handed** then make sure to see **Appendix 1** *after* you study this lesson. It spells out some important things you need to know about!

Chord Boxes

A **chord box** is a *visual representation* of the guitar fretboard showing you *where* to put your fingers in order to play a particular chord. They're also called **chord diagrams**. I'll use both names interchangeably throughout this book series.

Let's begin by looking at a blank chord box. Study the following diagram.

Each of the **vertical lines** represents one of the **guitar strings**. The one on the **left** is the **low E string**, the one on the right is the **high E string**. The other strings are the vertical lines in between.

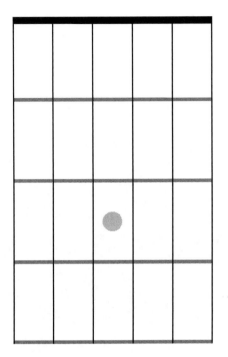

Make sure you grasp this, otherwise you'll be reading (and playing!) chords upside down.

The **horizontal lines** going across the chord box represent the **frets**. The top space between the frets is the 1st fret.

The next one is the 2nd fret, and so on. Study this first diagram to help this make sense.

In this second diagram the guitar strings and the frets have been labelled.

Study it to help everything I just described to you make perfect sense.

E   A   D   G   B   E

1

2

3

4

Understanding Where To Put Your Fingers

Markers on the chord box show you *where* to press down your fingers in order to play a certain chord. Usually this is shown using black or white circles.

Often these markers are labelled with a number telling you which finger to use (this is why knowing the fretting hand numbers matters).

In this book, finger position is shown by **black circles**. The **number** written *inside* the circle tells you which fretting hand finger to use.

Remember the Em chord from Lesson 2? Well, here is how it would be shown as a chord box:

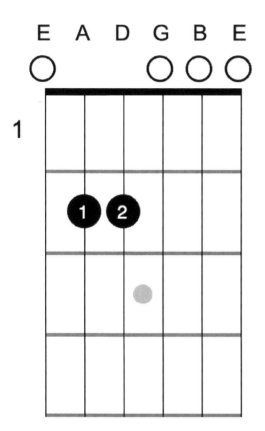

The black circle on the **A string** (2nd vertical line from the left) tells you to press down the A string inside the **2nd fret**. This marker is labelled with the number '1', suggesting that you use the **1st finger** on your fretting hand for this.

The black circle on the **D string** (3rd vertical line from the left) is shown in the **2nd fret** and labelled '2'. This tells you to press down the D string inside the 2nd fret with your **2nd finger**.

Notice that only the first fret is labelled, shown by a '1' on the left at the top of the diagram. It is not standard to number *every* fret in a chord diagram - often the frets are **not** numbered at all. When this is the case, you can assume the top fret in the diagram is the 1st fret.

The **grey circle** in the 3rd fret represents the fret marker you probably have at the 3rd fret on your guitar. These are sometimes shown on chord diagrams as well.

Playing and Leaving Out Open Strings

Chord boxes indicate which open strings, if any, to play as part of a chord. They also tell you which open strings we need to *leave out*.

Look at the Em chord diagram again. Notice the 'O' symbols above the low E, G, B and high E strings? These tell you to play these strings as open strings along with the fretted notes on the A and D strings. This effectively means that we play all six strings when we play this chord shape.

If any of these strings were marked with an 'X' instead of an 'O', it would indicate that we should *not* include that open string as part of the chord. We'll be seeing this in some of the chord shapes coming very soon.

Is this the only way chord shapes are shown in books and tutorials?

There are a few other methods for writing out chord shapes, but this is the most common method. Most other ways are variations on this basic idea anyway, so chances are you'll be able to decipher them too.

Exercise: Chord Box Familiarisation

1) Take a few minutes to relate the Em chord shape from Lesson 2 to the chord diagram in this lesson. Notice the way in which the diagram depicts the shape
2) Practice using the diagram to play the chord shape. Play the shape, take your fingers off the fretboard, then use the diagram to help you find the shape again
3) Do this several times - it will help you grasp the basics of reading chord boxes before we move on

That's all for Lesson 4: Ready To Move On?

Let's find out if you're ready for Lesson 5.

- Do you understand what the vertical and horizontal lines in a chord box represent?
- Do you understand how chord shapes are shown on the diagram?
- Do you understand how chord boxes indicate which fingers to use for playing a chord?
- Do you understand how open and omitted strings are shown on a chord diagram?

When you can honestly answer 'yes' to all of these questions , read on!

You've Completed Chapter 1 - Ready To Start Playing?

Well done for working through this introductory chapter and lessons. You now know:

- How to identify the basic parts of the guitar
- The names of the strings (E, A, D, G, B, E)
- How we use and number frets
- How to tune with an electronic tuner
- What notes and chords are
- How to read and understand chord boxes

Check-off each of these goals in the **chapter 1 checklist** found in your free **workbook** (see the very start of this book to find out how to download your copy). Doing this will help you decide when you're ready for chapter 2.

Everything we've talked about in this chapter is essential in order to get off to a good start on your journey of learning guitar, so read over it all again to make sure you have a solid understanding. Don't worry if some things seem a bit strange, once you begin to apply this knowledge it will soon become second nature.

When you're ready, I'll see you in the next chapter!

Chapter 2 – First Chords and Strumming Patterns (Lessons 5–8)

Now that you have the basic knowledge required to get started on the guitar, it's time to take your first steps towards playing music on the instrument. As before, work through each lesson in this chapter at your own pace, only moving to the next one when you are truly ready. This will ensure that you progressively and consistently build your knowledge and playing skills.

Ok, I think we're ready to begin. So grab your guitar, tune up, and let's dive into the first lesson.

Lesson 5 - 4 Essential Chord Shapes

In this lesson we're going to cover:

- 4 essential chord shapes (Em, G, D and C)
- A super-powerful exercise to use for learning and remembering chord shapes!

I'll be giving you chord diagrams for all the chord shapes we're going to cover in this lesson. These can also be found on the chord chart of your **free downloadable workbook**. See the start of this book to find out how to download your copy.

Ok, let's get started.

Golden Rule: 3 Things You MUST Know for Any Chord Shape

There are 3 crucial things you *must* know about any chord shape you learn:

1) The chord **shape** (where to put your fingers)
2) The chord **name** (e.g. D, Am, C etc.)
3) Which strings **are *not* played** as part of the chord (if any)

Remember to memorise all three of these things *every time* you learn a new chord shape - they are all *extremely* important.

Revisiting The Em Chord

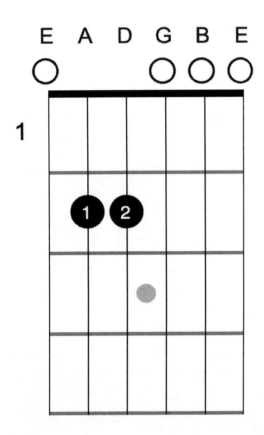

You saw this chord shape in chapter 1, but let's just have a bit of a reminder.

Make the Em chord shape on your guitar and give it a strum with a pick/thumb/finger to hear the sound. Don't worry if your chord shape or strumming don't sound perfect right now - we'll be looking at some things to help very soon.

Don't forget, you can see this chord shape demonstrated in the **Em Chord Demo video.** It's in the **Chord Shape videos** section at **start-guitar.com**

How To Learn Chord Shapes: The 'Throwing-Away Exercise'

This exercise is one of the **most important** things I want to share with you in this book. I've used it to help *thousands* of guitar players, and I think it's the fastest and easiest way to learn *any* new chord shape.

You can read about the exercise below or see me demonstrate it in the **Throwing-Away Exercise Demonstration video** at the website: **start-guitar.com** (you'll find it within the **Volume 1 videos** section).

In case you can't access the video, here's a description of the exercise as applied to the Em chord. Make sure to watch the video later to see it demonstrated, it will help make this description clearer.

1) Play the Em chord shape on your guitar
2) **Look** at the chord shape. Take in all the visual details of the shape
3) Continue looking until you have a 'mental snapshot' of what the chord shape looks like
4) **'Throw-Away'** the chord shape! Simply take your hand away from the guitar neck
5) **Visualise** the chord shape on the fretboard *as if* **you were playing it**
6) When you can clearly see the chord shape on the fretboard, play it again
7) Repeat this 5-6 times

When you perform this exercise you're *injecting* the visual elements of the shape directly into your memory. This helps your fingers quickly learn how to play it. The throwing-away exercise really is a powerful learning method, so make sure you *always* use it.

Quick Exercise - 'Throwing-Away' the Em Chord

Use the throwing-away exercise to thoroughly learn the Em chord shape right now. When you know it, we'll move onto the next chord shape.

Learning the G Chord

Here's how you play a G major chord. Remember, this is normally written simply as **G**.

You can see this chord shape demonstrated on the **Chord Shape videos** page at **start-guitar.com**

You should be playing:

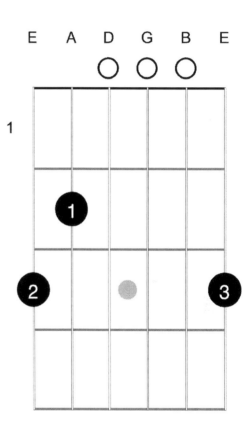

1) The **low E string** in the **3rd fret** with your **2nd finger**
2) The **A string** in the **2nd fret** with your **1st finger**
3) The **high E string** in the **3rd fret** with your **3rd finger**
4) The **D, G and B strings** as **open** strings

Pro Tip: The fretting hand needs to stretch a bit to play this shape. Try to keep your hand relaxed and loose to help with this. Most people don't find this stretch difficult after a little practice.

Quick Exercise - 'Throwing-Away' the G Chord

Use the throwing-away exercise to thoroughly learn the G chord shape. See the instructions we used for learning the Em chord if you need a reminder of what to do. When you know G thoroughly, move onto the next chord shape.

Learning the D Chord

The next chord we'll learn is *D major*, normally just called **D**. The shape is shown in the following chord diagram.

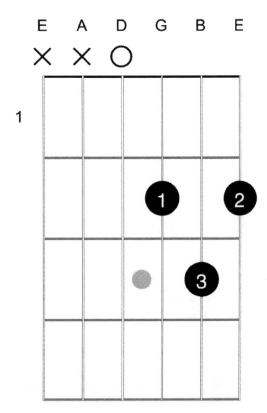

Notice how the low E and A strings are marked with an 'X' - this tells you that these strings need to be **missed out** when playing the chord shape - simply avoid striking them when you strum it.

If it helps, you can see the D shape demonstrated on the **Chord Shape videos** page at **start-guitar.com**

Use the chord diagram to play the D chord shape on your guitar now.

You should be playing:

1) The **G string** in the **2nd fret** with your **1st finger**
2) The **B string** in the **3rd fret** with your **3rd finger**
3) The **high E** in the **2nd fret** with your **2nd finger**
4) The **D string** is played as an **open** string
5) The low **E and A** strings are **not played**!

Check your chord alongside these instructions and strum it to hear the sound. Remember *not* to strum the low E and A strings!

Quick Exercise - 'Throwing-Away' the D Chord

Use the throwing-away exercise to thoroughly learn the D chord shape. Do this exercise over and over for several minutes.

Learning the C Chord

Now we'll learn to play **C** (or *C major*). The diagram is shown here, notice how we're leaving off the low E string.

To see this chord demonstrated see the **Chord Shape videos** page at **start-guitar.com**

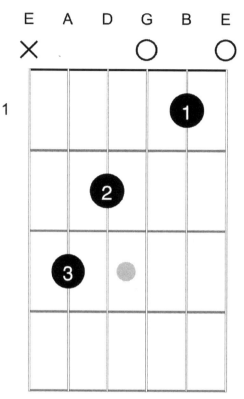

Check your C chord now, you should be playing:

1) The **A string** in the **3rd fret** with your **3rd finger**
2) The **D string** in the **2nd fret** with your **2nd finger**
3) The **B string** in the **1st fret** with your **1st finger**
4) The **G** and **high E** strings as **open** strings
5) The **low E string** is **not played**

Pro Tip: The C shape requires your fretting hand to stretch. Don't be put off if this feels difficult, persevere and you'll soon find that this becomes easier. Try to keep your fingers on their tips too!

Quick Exercise - 'Throwing-Away' the C Chord

Use the throwing-away exercise to thoroughly learn the C chord. Do this for several minutes. Persevere if the stretch is a bit tricky, keeping your hand as relaxed as possible, this can really help.

Quickfire Lesson: What To Do About Sore Fingers!

If your fingers are sore from playing the guitar, then you're definitely not alone - *all* guitar players experience this at some time! With regular practice the skin on your fingertips soon toughens up, but to start with, it can be uncomfortable.

So, what can you do?

1) Accept that sore fingertips are totally normal and allow your fingers time to toughen up
2) Avoid overly long practice sessions, they might make your fingertips too sore to play at all
3) Try short but frequent practice sessions to help build finger toughness

As I mentioned before, you can also try dabbing a little **salt water** on your fingertips before you go to bed each night. It soaks into the skin and hardens it up. I've found this helpful if my fingertips ever lose their toughness.

The most important thing is just to *keep going*. Do this, and sore fingertips will soon be a thing of the past.

That's all for Lesson 5: Ready To Move On?

- Do you understand the throwing-away exercise and how to use it to learn chords?
- Can you confidently play the Em chord?
- Can you confidently play the G chord?
- Can you confidently play the D chord?
- Can you confidently play the C chord?

If you haven't reached all these goals yet, just spend a little longer on this lesson. Then when you're ready, move on to Lesson 6.

Lesson 6 - Rhythm and Strumming Basics

In this lesson we're going to cover:

- 3 super-important rhythmic concepts
- Strumming technique basics
- Common patterns to use for strumming practice

Even the greatest sounding chords tend to count for nothing unless they're played with a solid rhythmic feel. This is why developing your understanding and sense of rhythm is so crucial. So, let's begin!

Essential Rhythmic Concepts

Let's look at some simple things you need to know about rhythm. We'll build on these in subsequent lessons, but it's important to get these basics in place first.

Rhythmic Feel and 'Groove'

Think of **feel** and **groove** as the rhythmic *life*, or *soul* of the music. This is what makes music *sound like* music, instead of just a load of odd, disconnected sounds. When people hear music and feel the urge to tap their foot, dance, or move their body in another way, they are responding to the rhythmic groove the music has built into it.

Feeling the 'Beat'

The **beat** is like the rhythmic heartbeat of a piece of music. When you clap your hands in time with a song, you're clapping in sync with the beat. The beat is like the *rhythmic pulse* underlying the whole song.

Stop reading for a moment, and listen to any piece of music. Can you hear the beat? Listening to the drummer in the song can make it easier. Try this with a few different songs. Don't over-analyse it, just try to *feel* and *hear* the beat.

Counting Beats and Time Signatures

In most music the beat is counted in groups of **four**.

To put it another way, you would *not* usually count a series of beats: *1,2,3,4,5,6,7,8,9,10,11,12* etc.

Instead, we'd count them as a *series* of groups of 4 beats: *1,2,3,4 - 1,2,3,4 - 1,2,3,4* etc.

The technical name for grouping the beat in this way is *four-four*. This is often written as **4/4**.

You may have seen the 4/4 symbol written at the start of a piece of music or on a song sheet? Typically it is written on the **stave**, this is what we call the system of 5 horizontal lines music is written on. You *don't* need to know *anything* about reading music to use this book, but at least try to remember what the stave is.

In the following image you can see the stave. The 4/4 symbol has been circled:

The 4/4 symbol is an example of a **time signature**. This tells a musician how to count the beat of the song so that it sounds the way it should.

This is a very basic way of explaining time signatures, but it will do for now. Later we'll go into more detail on this topic, for now, just remember that we normally count the beat in groups of four and that the technical name for this is 4/4 time.

Are all songs in 4/4 time?

Not *all* songs are in 4/4, but most are.

What's that squiggly symbol to the left of the time signature?

This is a **treble clef** sign and it's often shown at the start of a piece of music. It only matters if you're reading written music notation, which we're not, so get used to seeing a treble clef on a song sheet, but don't worry about what it means.

Quick Quiz

1) What do we mean by the beat?
2) How do we normally count the beat?
3) What's it called when we count the beat in groups of four?
4) What is the most common time signature?

Answers: 1) The beat is the **rhythmic pulse** of the music. 2) It's most common to count and feel the beat in **groups of 4**. 3) Counting beats in groups of four is called **four-four** time, written **4/4**. 4) The most common time signature is **4/4**.

Strumming Basics

Strumming is when we strike the strings to produce the sound of a chord. Most of the time we strum some sort of rhythmic pattern, so strumming is used to both sound the chord and create a rhythmic feel/groove.

A *strumming pattern* is the name guitarists use to describe the rhythm they are strumming on the guitar. Learning some specific strumming patterns is a great way to get started with strumming, but be aware that most experienced players *don't* rely on set strumming patterns - they'll just *instinctively* play something which fits the song they're playing. With time and practice you'll most probably develop this ability too!

There are some important things you need to know if you want to become comfortable strumming. The easiest way for you to learn about these is to see them demonstrated – so I've presented this information to you in a video lesson.

In the video we'll cover:

- Strumming with a pick/plectrum
- How to hold the pick
- Hand position, strumming action, and other important strumming guidelines
- Common strumming mistakes to watch out for
- Strumming with the thumb

… and much more!

If you can, watch the **Strumming Technique Basics video** at **start-guitar.com** to learn about all these points and more before you continue. You'll find it in the **Volume 1 videos** section of the website.

Video Summary

Hopefully you found the video lesson helpful. Watch it as many times as necessary to get everything you need from the lesson. If you are not able to watch it right now, make sure to check it out later. In the meantime, let's look at the main points from the video:

- How you grip the pick is a personal choice. Copy my grip to begin with, it works for most people. You can always modify it later if you want to
- Don't grip the pick too tightly (it causes tension) or strum with too much pick (it gets in the way)
- We use down strums and up strums (although we'll be focusing on down strums to begin with)
- Strumming with the thumb can work for some people - but in my experience as a teacher, using the pick is generally a better method

When it comes to the strumming action try to remember the following points from the video:

- Keep your strumming hand as close to the strings as you can
- Strum roughly halfway over the soundhole on your guitar
- Try to keep your hand, wrist, elbow and arm as relaxed as possible as you strum
- Strum from the wrist. Avoid excessive arm/elbow motion
- Try to avoid bending your wrist in 'towards' the guitar

Persevere with these guidelines and they'll soon begin to form a natural part of how you strum the guitar. Make sure to follow them all as you work through the strumming patterns coming next!

Exercise: Two Common Strumming Patterns

Let's examine some common strumming patterns. We'll only use down strums for now - in later lessons we'll explore using up strums as well.

It's really important to see and hear both these patterns to check you're on the right track. **Watch** the **Two Common Strumming Patterns video** to see both these patterns being demonstrated. You'll find this video in the **Volume 1 videos** section at: **start-guitar.com**

Strumming Pattern 1

The following strumming pattern is 4 beats long. We're simply strumming the chord once on each beat using a down strum.

This pattern may be simple, but it's surprisingly common. It's also a *great* way to train yourself to clearly hear and feel the beat (a super-important skill to develop!). We could write the pattern out as shown in the following diagram.

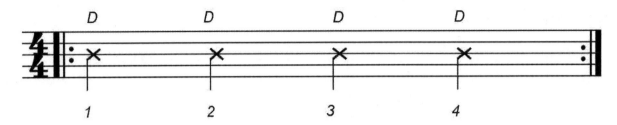

Let's look at how to understand the strumming pattern written out in this way.

- Each of the strums is shown as an 'X' on the **stave** (remember, the *stave* is the system of 5 lines we write music and strumming patterns on)
- Above each strum you can see a letter '**D**'. This is *my* way of easily telling you to use a down strum (it may be written differently in other books)
- A count of four under the pattern is there to help you see how the strums correspond to each of the four beats in the bar

We could count this strumming pattern: *1,2,3,4*

This represents the rhythmic pulse of the 4 beats. Let's have a go at playing this pattern now.

1) Count '*1,2,3,4*' slowly and evenly
2) Strum any chord shape softly but firmly on each beat. Count with your voice as you strum the chord
3) Loop the pattern round on a single chord shape in this way. Make sure to practice doing this with each of the chord shapes covered in Lesson 5

This strumming pattern uses **quarter notes**. Remember this phrase, it will be explained shortly.

Strumming Pattern 2

We don't always strum just *once* on each beat - if we did then the rhythms we played would soon get pretty boring. To make things more interesting, let's look at strumming twice on a beat.

In the following pattern we're doing *two* down strums on beat 3. Look carefully at beat 3 and you can see the two strums written, they're joined together to show you that they are simply one of the beats divided into two equal halves. We can count this strumming pattern: *1, 2, 3 and 4*.

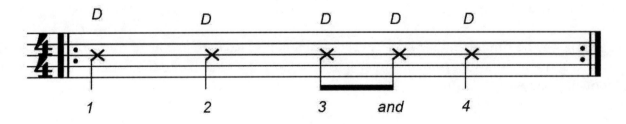

Let's play this pattern now:

1) Count '1,2,3 *and* 4' so that you capture the sound of the rhythm you're going to strum
2) Once you've established the count, strum any chord softly but firmly along to it. Remember to only use down strums for now
3) Loop the pattern round on a single chord shape. Repeat this for each chord shape from Lesson 5

Playing on the 'and' or second half of a beat is often described as playing on the '**off-beat**'. For example, in strumming pattern 2 we are strumming on the *off-beat of beat 3* (the 'and' of beat 3). Remember this terminology, we'll be referring to it throughout this book.

Reminder: As you practice both of these strumming patterns, follow the strumming guidelines from earlier:

- Keep the strumming hand relaxed, loose and close to the strings
- Your grip on the pick should be relaxed but controlled, with just a *tiny* bit of pick showing
- Strum with enough force to sound the chord, but not *too* hard
- Remember to miss off any unwanted strings when necessary (on C and D chord shapes)

Quick Theory Lesson: Note Values, Quarter Notes and Eighth Notes

In music we describe how long a sound lasts for as its **value**.

The value of a note or chord is expressed in terms of **how many beats** it sounds for. Something lasting for multiple beats has a *greater* value than something which only lasts for one beat or a fraction of a beat.

A sound which lasts for **1 beat** has the value of a **quarter note**.

Look back at **strumming pattern 1**. Each strum lasts for **1 beat**. We could say that we're strumming *quarter notes* when we play this pattern because we're playing a series of strums, each of which sounds for a single beat. Each strum has the value of a quarter note.

When we split a quarter note (lasting 1 beat) into two *equal* parts we get **eighth notes (8th notes)**. A single 8th note has a value or duration of *half* a beat. In **strumming pattern 2** you are playing two eighth notes on beat 3. On beats 1, 2 and 4 you're playing quarter notes. Study the next diagram to see this.

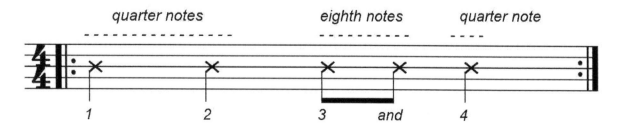

Don't be put off if this is a bit confusing, it's not super-important right now and it will make more sense as you work with different strumming patterns throughout the rest of this series.

That's all for Lesson 6: Ready To Move On?

Let's check if you're ready for the next lesson:

- Do you understand what is meant by rhythmic feel, groove, beat and time signature?
- Are you familiar with the strumming guidelines and techniques and have you been applying them?
- Can you confidently play strumming pattern 1 on each of the chord shapes from Lesson 5?
- Can you confidently play strumming pattern 2 on each of the chord shapes from Lesson 5?
- Do you have a basic understanding of what is meant by value, quarter note and eighth note?

If not, spend a little longer on this lesson. But if you're ready, let's move on to Lesson 7.

Lesson 7 - Three More Essential Chord Shapes

Welcome back! In this lesson we're going to expand and consolidate your knowledge of chord shapes. This is an important step and will help you progress through the next group of lessons. We're going to cover:

- Chord shapes for E, A and Am
- How to easily remember all the chord shapes studied so far
- Tips to get your chord shapes sounding top-notch!

Ok, let's get started.

Learning the A Chord

This next chord diagram shows you how to play A major. Normally we'd just call this chord **A**.

Using the chord box, play the shape on your guitar. You should be:

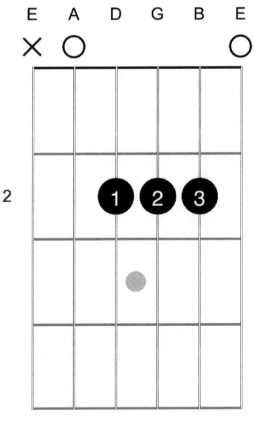

1) Playing the **D string** in the **2nd fret** with your **1st finger**
2) Playing the **G string** in the **2nd fret** with your **2nd finger**
3) Playing the **B string** in the **2nd fret** with your **3rd finger**
4) Playing the **A** and **high E strings** as **open** strings
5) **Missing out** the **low E** string when strumming the chord

Check your chord alongside these instructions, then strum to hear the sound.

Pro Tip: Fitting all three fingers into the 2nd fret can feel a bit of a squash. Try to keep your fingers on their ends and pressing on the fingertips, this helps to fit them into the fret. If you want to try using different fingers instead of those I'm suggesting then that's ok - with a bit of experimentation you might find an option you prefer.

You can see this chord shape demonstrated in the **Chord Shape videos** at **start-guitar.com**

Quick Exercise - 'Throwing-Away' the A Chord

Use the throwing-away-exercise to thoroughly learn the A chord. Do this for several minutes until you feel like you're familiar with this chord shape. If you need a reminder of how to use the throwing-away exercise see Lesson 5.

Learning the E Chord

The E major (or just **E**) chord uses all the strings and is a nice easy shape for your hand to make. The following diagram shows you how to play it:

Play the chord shape on your guitar. You should be playing:

1) The **A string** in the **2nd fret** with your **2nd finger**
2) The **D string** in the **2nd fret** with your **3rd finger**
3) The **G string** in the **1st fret** with your **1st finger**
4) The low **E**, **B** and **high E** strings as **open** strings

If it would help you to see this chord demonstrated then see the **Chord Shape videos** page at **start-guitar.com**

Quick Exercise - 'Throwing-Away' the E Chord

Now use the throwing-away exercise to learn the E chord. Do this for several minutes until you feel as though you thoroughly know how to play this shape.

Learning the Am Chord

The last chord we'll learn in this lesson is A minor, written as **Am**. The following diagram shows you how to play it, notice how the low E string needs to be left out of the chord:

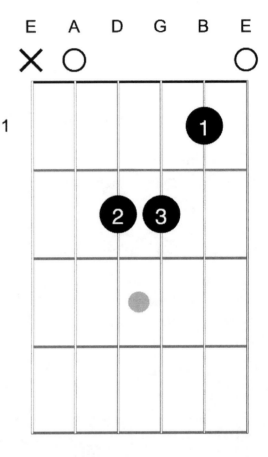

When playing Am you should be:

1) Playing the **D string** in the **2nd fret** with your **2nd finger**
2) Playing the **G string** in the **2nd fret** with your **3rd finger**
3) Playing the **B string** in the **1st fret** with your **1st finger**
4) Playing the **A** and **high E** strings as **open** strings
5) **Avoiding** the **low E** string

You can see this chord shape demonstrated on the **Chord Shape videos** page at **start-guitar.com**

Note: Visually this chord is similar to the E chord you learned a minute ago. You can use this to help you learn it, but **don't** get the shapes mixed up - this does often happen!

Quick Exercise - 'Throwing-Away' the Am Chord

Use the throwing-away exercise to thoroughly learn the Am chord. Keep doing this for several minutes.

Congratulations!

You now know seven of the most common chord shapes. Don't think that these shapes are *only* for beginners, they're used by virtually *all* guitar players, even those who have been playing for years. You might be wondering if there is an exercise you can use to help you remember these chords so you can easily find a shape when you need it? There is: the ***chord circle exercise***.

Exercise: The *Chord Circle Exercise*

This exercise is a simple way to practice all the chord shapes you've learned in a focused and time efficient way. Let's look at how it works.

The following diagram puts the names of the chords we've seen in a random order, arranged in a circle:

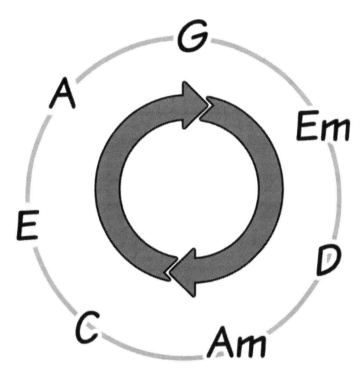

The idea is to start at the top and go in a *clockwise* direction (as shown by the arrows) around the circle playing each chord shape you come to. Don't worry about changing *between* the shapes or adding a strumming pattern, just play the chord shapes.

1) Play the chord at the top of the circle: **G**
2) Play the next chord: **Em**
3) Go to the next chord: **D**
4) Go to the next chord: **Am**
5) Continue round the circle playing each chord shape until you land back on G

The benefits of this exercise are:

1) The chord shapes aren't shown, so you're identifying the shapes using their **name** only (this is very important!)
2) By playing round the circle a few times you're practicing *all* the chord shapes you know in *just* a few minutes - the exercise is very time efficient
3) You instantly find out which chords you *really* know, and any you don't!

Now that you know how the chord circle works, we'll use a 3 step method to get amazing results with it.

Step 1: Play Around the Chord Circle 4-5 times

Don't stop for any problem chords - keep going, doing the exercise as well as you can for now.

Step 2: Respond To Feedback

Let's get some feedback on how you did:

- Which chords did you instantly know how to play?
- Which chords were you slower at finding?
- Which chords couldn't you remember at all?

Pay attention to this feedback - it shows you what you need to improve. Your goal is to be able to play *all* of these chord shapes *instantly*, you don't want any weaker chord shapes - they'll hold up your playing.

So now, focus on the *weak* chord shapes for about 5 minutes. I suggest using the throwing-away exercise for this. You might even write out a 'mini' chord circle containing *only* the problem chord shapes - this will really help you to fix them.

When you feel confident that the weaker chord shapes have improved, go to step 3.

Step 3: Play Round the Chord Circle Again

Play around the chord circle 3-4 times. Are you getting better results than the first time? Hopefully, you'll find the work you did in step 2 has made the weaker chords less of a problem.

Repeat this 3 step method round and round each time you practice - it only takes a few minutes and will help you to master all the chord shapes studied so far.

Pro Tip: This exercise is not about how quickly you can physically grab the chord shapes, it's about being 100% certain of what each shape is *called* and *exactly* how to play it - without any guesswork! Gaining speed at grabbing shapes accurately comes from practice and knowing *exactly* where to put your fingers on the guitar.

The chord circle diagram is also found in the **free downloadable workbook** which comes with this book. Print off the chord circle, put it on your wall or music stand, and it's there any time you want to work on your chord shapes. See the start of this book to find out how to download your workbook.

That's all for Lesson 7: Ready To Move On?

Let's check if you're ready for the next lesson:

- Can you play chord shapes for E, A and Am?
- Can you play all the way around the chord circle easily finding each of the seven chords?

If you're not quite there yet, that's fine - simply spend more time on this lesson. But when you're ready, move on to Lesson 8.

Lesson 8 - Chord Tips, Strumming Patterns and More!

This lesson aims to 'wrap-up' some of the ideas we've looked at in this chapter and prepare you to move on to the next set of lessons. We're going to look at:

- Tips for clean, clear, perfect sounding chord shapes!
- 'Bars' of music - what they are and how we use them
- Some more patterns for improving your strumming skills

Ok, let's begin.

Hand Position Tips for Top Sounding Chords

Let's look at some hand position tips to help you get your chords sounding tip-top. If you've been having trouble playing clean, clear chords then these tips should help.

Press With the Fingertips

- Press the strings down with your **fingertips**. This helps the fingers stay upright, making them less likely to interfere with any other strings in the chord shape
- It should feel like you are 'pinning' the strings to the fretboard when you press them down. This will help get clear sounding notes. To do this you're going to need short fingernails on your fretting hand, so **cut your nails** if necessary!

Thumb Position

- When playing chords my thumb normally goes somewhere between the back of the neck and the top side of the neck

- In my opinion (although some players may disagree) you don't want your thumb right behind or clamped stiffly over the top of the neck. I find both of these positions to be limiting
- Place your thumb in a position that feels comfortable to *you* - don't force it into a position which feels unnatural
- Use your thumb to help you maintain a stable, relaxed hand position

Push the Wrist Forward

- Check the palm of your hand isn't 'hugging' the back of the guitar neck. This causes the fingers to collapse onto the strings, instead of pressing the strings down firmly with the fingertips
- To help avoid the above, think about pushing your wrist *forward*. This helps put your fingers in a good playing position. Experiment with doing this and see if it helps

Summary

All of these hand position guidelines can be modified to suit your physicality and hand size and as long as you observe the basic principles you'll probably find them helpful. In my experience, with regular practice everyone soon finds a hand position which works for them. Remember, keep everything as relaxed as possible - some tension is needed, but not too much.

The following photo shows my hand position for playing an Am chord. Notice how:

- My fingers are on their tips, 'pinning' the strings to the fretboard (1)
- My thumb is sitting comfortably along the top of the neck (2)
- My wrist is pushing slightly forward rather than collapsing onto the back of the guitar neck (3)

Now apply these hand position guidelines to the chord shapes you know.

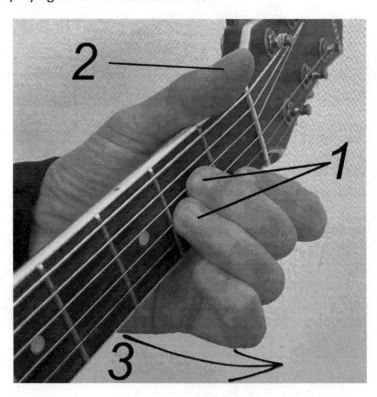

Do they result in better sounding chords? If so, notice what has helped and try to make doing it a habit!

Pro-Tip: Try picking across a chord shape **one string at a time**. Strumming all the strings together can conceal mistakes, but by playing the *individual* strings in a chord you can easily hear which notes are sounding clearly and which are not. You can then take action to improve the chord shape as necessary.

Chord FAQs

Let's look at some of the most common questions people ask about chords and chord shapes. If you've got a nagging chord question you'll hopefully find the answer in here somewhere.

My chord shapes sound dead and muffled. Why won't the strings ring out?

- Are you pressing the strings down hard enough - 'pinning' them to the fretboard?
- Are one or more fingers accidentally touching a string(s) in the chord shape and stopping it from sounding?
- Are your fingers falling a bit 'flat' or are they squarely on their tips?

I can't stretch my fingers enough to play some chord shapes. Are my hands too small to play them?

It's highly unlikely that the size of your hands is the problem here, you probably just need to spend more time training your hands to adopt positions they're not yet used to. Try the following tips to help:

- Don't avoid problem chord shapes - practice them the *most* so that you develop the necessary stretch
- Keep your fingers relaxed and loose as you reach for the chord shape - too much tension makes stretching more difficult
- Check if your guitar is too big for you. This might sound silly but I'm serious - for example some Spanish/classical guitars have very wide necks making them more difficult to play
- Ensure the guitar is not sitting too low on your lap/guitar strap - this makes stretching more difficult

I can't keep my fingers on their tips!

- Playing on the fingertips is harder with stretchy chord shapes like C - be patient!
- Check your thumb isn't in an awkward position and restricting your fingers
- Keep your thumb/hand loose and relaxed - avoid too much tension!
- Push your wrist gently forward as shown earlier. This can help get your fingers on their tips

I know the chord shapes but I don't know what they're called.

- You *must* know the shapes by name. Spend more time memorising the names
- Use the **chord circle exercise** to get used to associating the shapes with the names
- No magic fix here - just more work needed!

I just can't seem to remember the chord shapes - is it just me who has this problem?

- You might be working on *too many* shapes at once and getting them confused. Learn them one at a time, really nailing one chord shape before you move on to another
- It can take a while for the shapes to sink in, just be patient and keep doing the practice
- The **throwing-away exercise** and the **chord circle** can really help with this - use them
- Are you rushing? If so, slow down and methodically work through the shapes

I find some chord shapes so much easier than others - is this common?

Yes, some shapes are simply easier to play than others. For example, many players struggle with C when starting out.

Remember to:

- Patiently work on any tricky chord shapes. They don't need to be *perfect* right away - just give it some time
- Don't *avoid* the more difficult shapes, otherwise they'll never really improve!

My chords aren't improving fast enough!

It's easy to be impatient and become frustrated that we're not improving as fast as we would like (I'm just as guilty of this as anyone). As guitarists, we need to learn to be patient and just keep on doing the work!

So patiently follow my instructions, persevere, celebrate the small wins, and most importantly enjoy the journey.

Quick Theory Lesson: Bars and Chord Symbols

We've seen how most of the time we count beats in groups of **four**. This is called *four-four* time and is written **4/4**.

When writing out a song it's normal to arrange the music in **bars**. A bar is a small unit of the song and contains a certain number of beats.

When you see the 4/4 time signature in a piece of music it tells you that each bar represents a count of 4 beats. In other words, each bar is **4 beats long**. The following image shows the stave divided up into bars, each lasting for 4 beats, as shown by the 4/4 time signature:

Bars make it easy to follow the structure of a song by breaking it up into smaller chunks. Without them it would be like reading a book with no spaces between the words - just imagine how difficult this would make it to see where one word ended, where the next began, and to keep your place!

Chord names or **chord symbols** are written *inside* or *above* the bars. These are there to tell you which chord to strum for each bar. Study the following image:

In the above example each chord is played for one bar each. This means that you'd play:

G for **4 beats**, then **Em** for **4 beats**, then **D** for **4 beats**, then **C** for **4 beats**.

Study this explanation with the image to help you understand this concept. If it doesn't make total sense right now, don't worry - once you get used to using this system to play songs it will become second nature.

Quick Quiz

1) How many beats does a bar normally last for?
2) The most common time signature is 4/4. What does this tell us about each bar in a song?
3) What do we commonly see written inside or above each bar of a song?

Answers: 1) In most songs a bar lasts for 4 beats. 2) The common 4/4 time signature tells us that there are 4 beats in each bar. 3) Chord symbols are written in or above each bar. These tell you which chord shape to play for the duration of a particular bar in a song.

More Strumming Patterns

Let's look at two more strumming patterns to develop your strumming and rhythmic skills further. Doing this will be of great benefit when we start *combining* strumming and chords in the next chapter.

Be sure to listen to and see these strumming patterns demonstrated in the **More Strumming Patterns video** on the website which accompanies this book at **start-guitar.com.** You'll find the video in the **Volume 1 videos** section of the site.

Remember:

- Play both patterns using **down-strums** with the pick (up-strums will be covered later)
- Practice each pattern on a **single** chord for now
- Apply these patterns to each of the chord shapes in the **chord circle** (this is great strumming *and* chord shape practice!)

Strumming Pattern 1

With this pattern we're strumming quarter notes for beats 1 and 4. We're strumming 8th notes for beats 2 and 3, both on the beat and on the off-beat. We'd count this strumming pattern as '1, 2 *and*, 3 *and*, 4'. This is shown under the diagram.

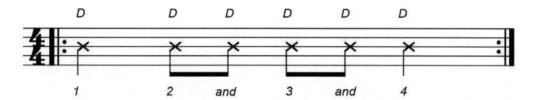

To get comfortable playing this pattern:

1) Count '1, 2 *and 3 and* 4' slowly and evenly. This represents the rhythm you're going to strum
2) Strum the rhythm softly but firmly on any chord shape. You may want to keep counting out loud to help you keep track of the rhythm
3) Repeat this exercise with other chord shapes

Strumming Pattern 2

In this next pattern we're strumming quarter notes on beats 1 and 2 and pairs of 8th notes on beats 3 and 4. Count this pattern as '1, 2, 3 *and*, 4 *and*'.

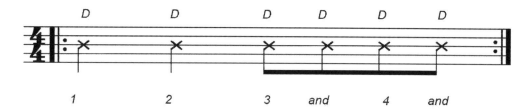

Practice this pattern now:

1) Count '1, 2 ,3 *and* 4 *and*' slowly and evenly
2) Strum the rhythm softly but firmly on any chord shape. Keep counting out loud to help you keep track of the rhythmic pattern
3) Repeat this exercise with various chord shapes

That's all for Lesson 8: Ready To Move On?

Let's find out if you're ready for the next lesson:

- Have you applied the tips covered in this lesson to improve the clarity of your chord shapes?
- Do you understand *bars* and how we use them when playing music?
- Can you confidently play the two strumming patterns from this lesson?

When you're able to do all these things you're ready to move on.

Congratulations: You've Reached the End of Chapter 2

Everything we've studied in this chapter has got you much closer to your goal of playing the guitar.

Having studied this chapter you:

- Can play chord shapes for Em, G, D, C, A, E, Am
- Know how to use the 'Throwing-Away' exercise for learning chord shapes
- Can use the chord circle to practice and remember chord shapes
- Understand rhythmic concepts like beats, time signatures, bars etc.
- Are aware of important strumming guidelines
- Can play 4 common strumming patterns using down-strums

Check-off each of these goals in the **chapter 2 checklist** found in your free **workbook**, this will help you see for sure if you're ready for chapter 3. If you don't have your workbook yet, see the start of this book to find out how to download your copy.

Don't underestimate the importance of what you've learned in this chapter - you can play an *insane* amount of music with *just* these chords and rhythms. Many people know little more than this and are still able to enjoy playing the guitar!

For this reason, I urge you to take your time working through this material. Go back over anything you need to revisit and get everything as good as you can before heading to the next chapter - it will be worth it in the long run.

Good luck and see you in chapter 3.

Chapter 3 – Starting To Make Music (Lessons 9–12)

Now that you've got some chord shapes and strumming patterns under your fingers it's time to put them together and start playing music. Learning to do this is the focus of this next set of lessons.

In this chapter you're going to learn:

- How to teach yourself to change smoothly between chord shapes
- How to learn to strum and change between chord shapes …at the *same* time!
- The basics of reading a song sheet
- How to play your first song

This is where things really start to get fun - and with a bit of practice you'll start to feel as though you can actually play something on the guitar!

Lesson 9 - Changing Between Chord Shapes

Watch any guitar player perform a song and they'll nearly always be changing *between* various chord shapes. They may start on G, change to D, switch to Em, and so on. Changing between chord shapes is a crucial skill to master because few (if any) songs use only *one* chord shape.

The trouble is that playing and strumming through a sequence of chords can be really challenging at first - we need to remember the chord shapes, switch between them, think which chord is next, *and* keep the strumming rhythm going …all at the same time. This takes some serious multi-tasking ability and it's no surprise that it can easily come crashing down!

I believe that the key is to start *really* simple, and that's exactly what we are going to do. To begin with we'll focus almost exclusively on the role of the fretting hand. When this hand is working well, we'll add strumming. In my experience this approach works best. We'll start by looking at three important chord changing principles which you need to know about.

Golden Rules: Chord Changing

To see these three concepts demonstrated watch the **Golden Rules of Chord Changing video**, it's in the **Volume 1 videos** section at **start-guitar.com**.

There are 3 crucial rules to remember when it comes to changing between chord shapes;

Rule #1: Be 100% *Certain* of Your Chord Shapes!

You can't move your fingers effortlessly to a new chord shape if you don't know *where* to move them to. Before you even *attempt* a chord change, make sure you are 100% certain of how to play the chord shapes you need to know. This seems obvious, but many people make this mistake.

Rule #2: Look Ahead!

Prepare for a chord change by **looking ahead** to where you're moving your fingers to. The idea is to 'see' the chord shape you are changing to **before** it's time to begin moving to it. Your aim is to **visualise** the chord shape you are moving to on the fretboard.

I've found this learning technique to be *incredibly* powerful. I think this is because:

- you're preparing for the chord change by *pre-programming* your fingers where to move to
- you're doing the thinking-part of the chord change in advance - when it's time to move your fingers you know *exactly* where you need to put them

Rule #3: Leave Fingers In Place When Possible!

Sometimes one or more fingers are in the same place for both chord shapes. When this is the case, don't move them - leave them in place. This can take a little bit of practice to get used to, but it makes some chord changes a lot easier to execute. So remember, only move fingers when necessary.

Remember each of these rules anytime you're working on chord changing - you'll find that they make a huge difference!

The Chords-Pairs Method

The idea behind the **chord pair method** is simple: take two chords and practice changing between them over and over. By focusing on and really nailing a particular chord change you'll perform it without difficulty *every time* you see it in a song. I've found working with **chord pairs** to be the fastest and most efficient way to master the common chord changes you need to be comfortable with, so let's look at some chord pairs now.

Important: If you go to the website which accompanies this book series, you'll find a **play-along video** for each of the chord pairs we are going to study. Playing along with me in these videos is a great way to perfect each chord pair. Check them out in the **Chord Pair videos** section at **start-guitar.com**.

The G to Em Chord Pair

Changing between G and Em is common and straightforward, so it's the perfect chord pair to begin with.

Here's a quick reminder of the chord shapes. 'Throw-away' each shape 4-5 times then follow the step-by-step method that follows.

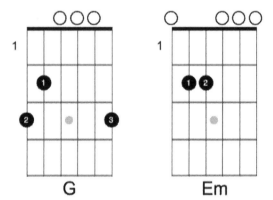

Step 1
Make the G chord shape with your fingers. Give it a strum if you want to.

Step 2
Whilst holding down the G chord shape, look carefully at the fretboard of your guitar. Imagine you can 'see' the Em chord shape. Don't rush this step - you need to clearly *visualise* the Em chord on the fretboard.

Step 3
When you can see the Em chord (and not before), slowly and smoothly move your fingers to play it. Don't rush or panic your fingers - keep them relaxed and calm. When you've got the Em shape pressed down, give it a strum. (**Tip** - your 1st finger is in the same place for *both* chords and **doesn't** need to move!)

Step 4

Now we'll return to G. Whilst holding the Em chord shape, *visualise* your fingers making the G chord shape. When you can see it, move your fingers to play G. Remember, keep the 1st finger in position, it doesn't need to move.

Step 5

Repeat this process for several minutes, changing backwards and forwards between each shape. Make your chord changing relaxed, accurate and unhurried. It's ok if it's not perfect to begin with, just keep going.

Remember: Practice this chord pair along with me using the **G to Em Chord Pair video** at **start-guitar.com**. It's in the **Chord Pair videos** section.

We could write the G to Em chord pair exercise like this:

G ↔ Em

The **double-arrows** represent changing back-and-forth between each shape to master this chord change. This is how I will write out some chord pairs from now on in this book.

Pro Tip: Change in both directions!

Notice how you're not only changing from G to Em - when you return to G you're practicing changing from Em to G, so this exercise will help you master **two** chord changes.

Always practice changing in both 'directions' between the shapes in a chord pair. This way you are mastering *two* changes with just *one* exercise. This is one of the things that makes this chord pair exercise such a powerful and time efficient practice method!

The A to Em Chord Pair

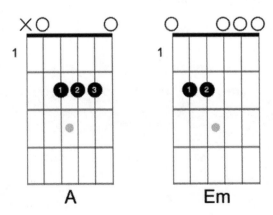

A ↔ Em

As before, start by 'throwing-away' each chord shape 4-5 times then follow the same step-by-step method we used for the previous chord pair.

Step 1
Make the A chord shape with your fingers. You can give it a strum if you want to.

Step 2
Holding the A chord shape, look at the fretboard and **visualise** the Em chord shape.

Step 3
When you can see the Em chord, slowly and smoothly move your fingers to play it. Give it a strum. (**Tip** - all your fingers need to move, but not by much - keep the finger movements as small as possible!)

Step 4
Whilst holding the Em chord shape, visualise the A chord shape. When you can see it, move your fingers to play A.

Step 5
Repeat the A - Em chord pair for a few minutes using this step-by-step method.

Remember: Practice this chord pair along with the **A to Em Chord Pair video** at **start-guitar.com**!

Is it important how fast I can change between the chords in a chord pair?

Quickly changing between chord shapes is not just about how fast you move your fingers - it's about efficiency and accuracy. Don't be tempted to *rush* chord pair exercises, switch between the chords slowly, smoothly and accurately. Do this, and the speed will come over time. Hurried and sloppy chord changing practice will not pay off - remember this as you practice your chord pairs!

That's all for Lesson 9: Ready To Move On?

Are you ready to move on to the next lesson?

- Do you know the 3 Golden Rules for changing chords?
- Do you understand how to do the chord pairs exercise? Make sure you do, we'll be using it a lot
- Can you confidently change between G and Em?
- Can you confidently change between A and Em?

When you can answer 'yes' to these questions you're ready to move on to the next lesson.

Lesson 10 - More Chord Pairs

This lesson will help you master some other common chord pairs and prepare you for your first song which we're going to look at in Lesson 12.

The chord changes I'm showing you are used *everywhere*, and you'll find them in literally *thousands* of well-known songs. This means that the skills you're learning now will help you to play many of the songs you might one day wish to play. Ok, let's get started.

Chord Pair Exercises

The G to D Chord Pair

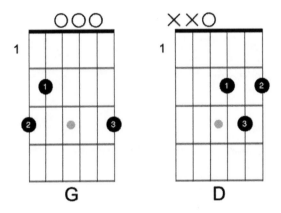

G ↔ D

We've already seen how to practice chord pairs so I won't go into great detail here. Use the following summary as a reminder if you need to.

- Play the first chord (G in this case)
- Look at the fretboard and *visualise* the chord you're changing to (D in this case)
- When you're ready, move slowly and accurately to the new chord
- Repeat the process to return to the first chord (G)

Remember: Practice along with the **G to D Chord Pair video** in the **Chord Pairs videos** section at **start-guitar.com** when you're ready.

The E to Am Chord Pair

This chord pair is one of the easiest because of how similar the shapes are.

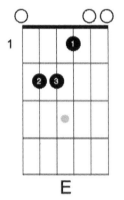 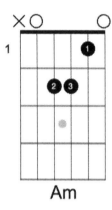

E ↔ Am

- Play the first chord (E)
- Look at the fretboard and visualise the chord you're changing to (Am)
- When you're ready, move slowly and accurately to the new chord
- Repeat the process to return to the first chord (E)

Remember: Practice along with the **E to Am Chord Pair video** at **start-guitar.com**.

The G to C Chord Pair

Changing between G and C is extremely common, so this is an important chord pair to master. It can be a bit tricky to start with, so persevere!

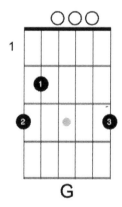 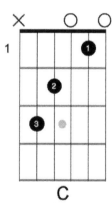

G ↔ C

- Play the first chord (G)
- Look at the fretboard and visualise the chord you're changing to (C)
- When you're ready, move slowly and accurately to the new chord
- Repeat the process to return to the first chord (G)

Remember: Practice along with the **G to C Chord Pair video** at **start-guitar.com**.

Chord Pair Summary

We've now seen 5 chord pairs:

- G and Em
- A and Em
- G and D
- E and Am
- G and C

I suggest that you work out a short practice routine to help you master these changes. For example:

- Practice each chord pair non-stop for 2 minutes (10 minutes in total)
- Practice each chord pair 5 times then move to the next one (do this for 10 minutes in total)

Create your own routine if you'd prefer, the idea is simply to have something in place to help you consistently and methodically work through each of these important chord pairs. Practice your routine each day (twice if you can!) and you'll soon be ready for the next lesson.

That's all for Lesson 10: Ready To Move On?

Can you confidently perform the following chord pairs?

- G and Em
- A and Em
- G and D
- E and Am
- G and C

If not, spend a while longer on getting them as good as you can. Then when you feel ready move on to the next lesson.

Lesson 11 - Chord Changing and Strumming (At the Same Time!)

In this lesson we'll look at strumming and changing chords *together*. Of course, this is what you'll be doing most of the time you're playing the guitar. If you've done your homework and can perform the chord pairs from Lessons 9 and 10 then this will likely be easier than you think. We'll begin this lesson with some important principles you need to know.

Golden Rules: Strumming and Chord Changing

Rule #1 - Don't Overthink the Strumming!

Focus *most* of your attention on the **fretting hand** change between the chord shapes, this is where problems normally happen. Try not to think about the strumming too much - just relax and try to let it happen. Trust me, with practice this will become easier than it might seem to you now!

Rule #2 - Keep Looking Ahead

It's *super-important* to keep **looking for the chord shape** you're changing to as you approach it. I suggest you get used to looking at your strumming hand as *little* as possible - with a bit of practice this will soon feel quite natural. People often focus all their attention on the strumming and the chord changing falls apart as a result.

Rule #3 - The Strumming Hand MUST NOT WAIT for the Fretting Hand!

This rule is *really* important. The job of the strumming hand is to keep a steady rhythmic pattern going. It MUST NOT STOP! Think about the fretting hand keeping-up with the strumming hand, *rather* than the other way round.

I always tell my students to keep the strumming going *even* if the new chord isn't in place yet. I know this sounds crazy, but there's a good reason. You see, if the strumming hand *doesn't* wait for the fretting hand, you train the fretting hand to get *really* good at keeping up! Conversely, if you allow the strumming hand to compensate for slow chord changing, then nothing really improves. It's *really* important that you try to stick to this principle, even though it might sound counterintuitive.

To make it easier to build this habit:

- Start with *very* simple strumming patterns
- Start with the chord pairs you find the *easiest*

- Give yourself lots of 'looking ahead' time. This will help you clearly visualise the chord you are changing to without feeling rushed

Remember each of these 3 rules - they'll help you to avoid the most common mistakes people make and get you strumming and changing chords together much sooner.

Strumming Chord Pairs

Let's look at how to start strumming and changing chords at the same time using the G to Em chord pair as an example.

It's important to start with *very simple* strumming so we'll use the basic quarter note strumming pattern that you played in Lesson 6. The strumming pattern will be played *twice* on G before changing to Em. It is then played twice on Em. As before, we'll play the pattern with down strums.

Written out the exercise looks like this:

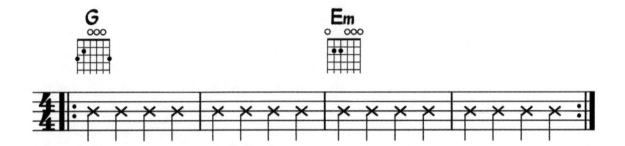

Repeat Marks

The dots at the start and end of the exercise (:) are **repeat marks**. These common musical symbols simply tell you to repeat the music *between* the dots again. In other words, once you've finished strumming Em, change back to G and repeat the exercise.

With an exercise like this one, repeat marks tell you to loop the exercise round as many times as you want to. In a song type setting, they will be more specific, telling you exactly how many times to repeat something (we'll see this later).

We use repeat marks to avoid writing the same thing out multiple times. This makes it easier for someone to read a song sheet because there is less information to process and follow. Get used to recognising and using repeat marks, they're very common.

Let's return to the exercise now and try the G to Em chord pair with strumming.

Step 1: Start on G. Strum the quarter note strumming pattern *twice* (you'll perform 8 strums in total). Go as slowly as you like but make sure a *rhythmic pulse* can be clearly heard. As you strum, look on the fretboard and visualise the Em chord shape so that when it's time to change, you know exactly where your fingers are going.

Step 2: If you've been looking ahead as you strum, then getting to Em should be easy. As soon as you execute the final strum in the second bar, smoothly move to the Em chord - keep the strumming going - the chord change should **not** affect the rhythm!

Step 3: Keep the strumming going on the Em chord now. As you do, start visualising the G chord on the guitar neck. Play the strumming pattern twice on Em (2 bars in total).

Step 4: As soon as you execute the final strum on the Em chord, smoothly return to the G chord - keep the strumming going! Repeat the whole exercise, continuously changing between G and Em whilst strumming.

Practice this exercise until it begins to feel comfortable. If you make a mistake or get lost, don't worry - just pick yourself up and carry on.

Spending 2 bars on each chord is a good place to begin, but once you've got the hang of this you can try playing the strumming pattern *once* on each chord (4 strums on each). Follow the same method as before, remembering to observe all the important rules and guidelines we've discussed.

When written down this exercise looks as follows:

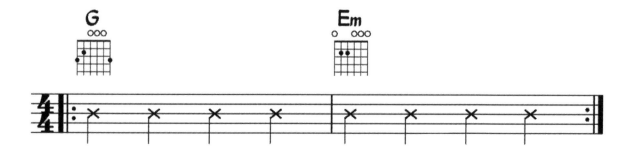

Performance Tips

- Don't worry if these exercises feel difficult to start with, just keep working on them. With practice you'll soon get used to doing what at first seems like lots of things at the same time! This is why it's so important to start with *easy* chord pairs and *easy* strumming. Once you learn the skill you can then transfer it to other chord pairs

- Remember to keep the strumming going, no matter what! If you do this, your fretting hand *will* learn to keep up, even if it doesn't feel like it can at first

Exercise: Basic Strumming (All Chord Pairs)

Apply the method we just studied to all 5 chord pairs seen so far. Start with the 2 bar strumming pattern on each chord. When you can do this, practice the exercise with the 1 bar strumming pattern. As you do this, remember to follow *all* the guidelines and principles we've discussed.

- G and Em
- A and Em
- G and D
- E and Am
- G and C

Introducing More Complex Strumming

Now we'll apply the other strumming pattern from Lesson 6. Don't let the slightly more complex strumming pattern throw you, do exactly what you did with the simpler pattern in the previous exercise:

- Keep the strumming going through the chord change
- Keep your eyes mostly on the fretting hand (not the strumming hand)
- Look for the new chord shape as the change approaches
- Go slow and get it right - rushed, uneven, out of time strumming and changing will not benefit you

Let's take the A-Em chord pair. If we play the strumming pattern *twice* on each chord it looks like this:

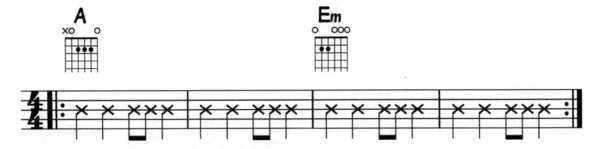

Remember, for now we're only using down-strums with the pick when playing these strumming patterns.

When you can comfortably play this exercise, perform the strumming pattern *once* on each chord as shown in the following image:

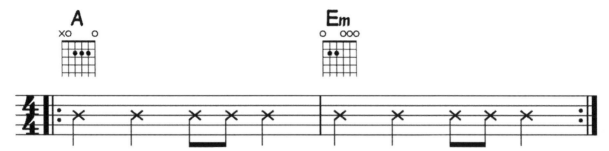

Remember all the important points we've covered as you work through the following exercise.

Exercise: More Complex Strumming (All Chord Pairs)

Apply the more challenging strumming we just studied to all 5 chord pairs seen so far. Begin by playing the strumming pattern *twice* on each chord. When you can do this, play the pattern *once* on each chord. Good luck!

- G and Em
- A and Em
- G and D
- E and Am
- G and C

That's all for Lesson 11: Ready To Move On?

We've covered some *really* important material in this lesson, some of which will directly translate into playing your first song in Lesson 12. Before moving on, make sure you can perform both of the exercises in this lesson on the following chord pairs:

- G and Em
- A and Em
- G and D
- E and Am
- G and C

When you've achieved this, I'll see you in Lesson 12!

Lesson 12 - Your First Song - Gone Sailing

In this lesson we'll look at your first song: *Gone Sailing*. This will give you the chance to put what you've learned so far together into a musical performance.

We'll also examine a simple method you can use to learn almost *any* song you want to play, plus cover a load of other super-important tips and concepts along the way.

You'll want to check out the **Gone Sailing Demo video** before you begin this lesson. You'll find it in the **Volume 1 videos** section at **start-guitar.com**.

Also on the site you can also visit the **About the Songs in the Series** page to see which famous song *Gone Sailing* is based on (in case you can't guess!).

I'm really excited to help you play your first song, so grab your guitar and we'll get started!

Understanding and Reading a Song Sheet

A **song sheet** tells you what you need to know to play a particular song - things like:

- Which chords to play
- When to play them
- How long to play them for
- The overall structure of the song and sections it uses (e.g. introduction, verse, chorus etc.)

Sometimes a song sheet also gives you a suggested rhythm or strumming pattern to play and/or the words to the song.

Having a basic understanding of how to read a song sheet will not only help you use this book series, it will also make it possible for you to use basic song sheets to learn other songs too.

Let's look at *Gone Sailing* written out in a basic song sheet format.

Don't worry if some things are confusing, this example is just so you can see what a song sheet looks like, we'll break everything down in a second.

'Gone Sailing'

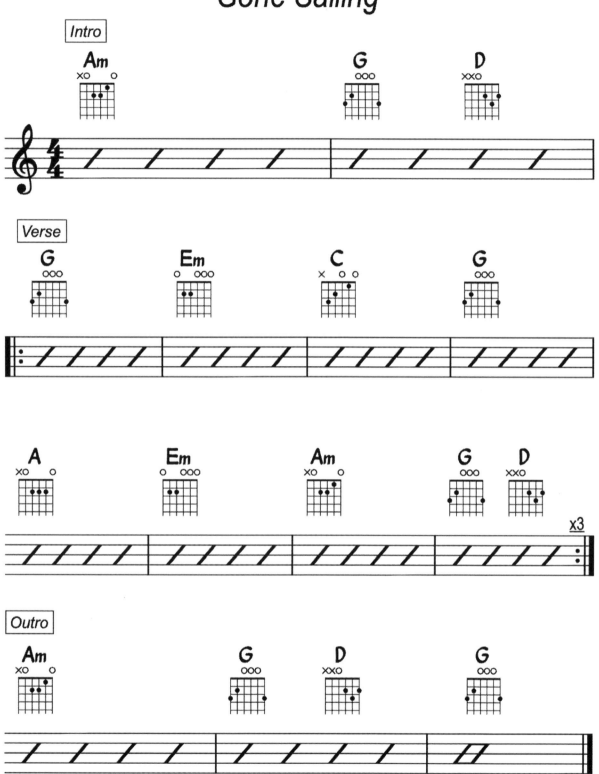

Let's look at what this song sheet is actually telling you.

Look at the section labelled **intro** (short for *introduction*). Understanding this section will teach you *most* of what you need to know:

- The **4/4 time signature** written at the start tells us that each bar lasts for **4 beats** (see Lesson 6 if you need a reminder on this). Sometimes a time signature is not shown, in which case it's normally safe to assume the song is in 4/4 time
- The '**slashes**' on the stave give a rough representation of the beat. Notice how there are 4 slashes in each bar? This is because each bar contains 4 beats
- **Chord symbols** (chord names) are written above the stave. I've provided the chord shapes too, but often you'll only be given the chord symbol
- The **Am** chord lasts for a whole bar. We can tell this because it is the only chord symbol given for that bar. This means you need to play it for 4 beats
- In the 2nd bar there are two chords: **G** and **D**. The 4 beats in this bar are split equally between them with each chord lasting for 2 beats
- Notice how the intro is simply the final 2 bars of the verse chord progression

After the intro we play the **verse** chord sequence several times. Refer to the verse on the song sheet.

- The repeat signs (see Lesson 11) at the beginning and end of the verse tell you to repeat the verse chord progression again. The **x3** at the end of the verse adds to this instruction, telling you to play the chord sequence three times in total*
- After playing the verse three times you play the **outro** to close out the song (look at the complete song sheet to see the outro)

(* If the x3 instruction was not there you would assume the verse was only repeated once. This means you would play it twice in total)

Song Sheets and Strumming

Sometimes a song sheet may give you a strumming pattern to play (this is something we'll be seeing later). Other times, it's left up to the player to choose a strumming rhythm which they think will work for the song, a skill which becomes easier with experience. In the case of *Gone Sailing* I'll be giving you some specific strumming patterns to use later.

Using Chord Pairs to Master Any Song

Study the chord sequence used in *Gone Sailing*. Can you work out which chord changes you need to be able to execute to play the song?

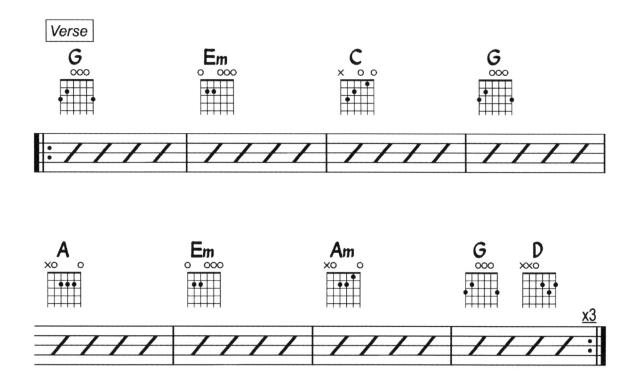

Did you manage to work them out? We need to change from **G to Em** in bars 1 and 2 and from **Em to C** in bars 2 and 3. Then we need to change from **C to G** in bars 3 and 4.

We could write these out as chord pairs:

G-Em   Em-C   C-G

If we continue through the remainder of the verse we also get the following chord pairs:

G-A
A-Em
Em-Am
Am-G
G-D
D-Am (used when transitioning from verse to outro)

By practicing each of these chord pairs we can build the skills we need to play the song well.

Pro Tip: When learning a new song it *really* pays off to work out which chord changes you need to be able to perform and master each of them. I highly recommend you do this *every* time you start working on a new song - you're almost guaranteed to get better results than if you jump straight in and try to play the song without any experience.

Don't forget this pro tip!

Exercise: Gone Sailing Chord Pairs

We'll apply the practice methods used in Lessons 10-11 to each of the chord pairs used in *Gone Sailing*. You've seen some of these chord pairs already, the others are new. Here's a reminder of how to work with chord pairs:

- Practice each pair without strumming (fretting hand only)
- Add strumming when you're ready (use patterns from earlier or make up your own)
- Keep the rhythm steady and smooth - don't rush!

Here are the *Gone Sailing* chord pairs again - practice them in the way I've described.

G-Em	G-A	Am-G
Em-C	A-Em	G-D
C-G	Em-Am	D-Am

Remember: Practice each of these along with me using the **Chord Pair videos** at **start-guitar.com**! For C-G, look at the **G&C Chord Pair video**.

Exercise: Gone Sailing Strumming Patterns

We'll use two simple strumming patterns when we perform the song. To see both of these demonstrated watch the **Gone Sailing Strumming video** at **start-guitar.com** in the **Volume 1 videos** section.

Strumming Pattern 1

This pattern is using 2 down strums per bar - on beats 1 and 3.

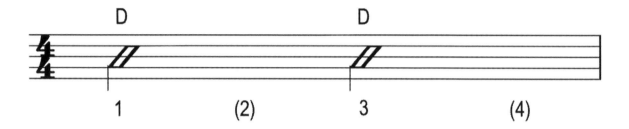

A strum which sounds for a half a bar or 2 beats could be described as a **half note**. This is often shown as a 'hollow' forward-slash as in the previous example.

Let's practice this strumming pattern now. Simply strum this pattern on any of the chord shapes used in this song. The pattern may be easy, but aim to get the chords ringing out clearly.

Strumming Pattern 2

This pattern is like we saw in Lesson 6. We're simply performing a down strum on each beat of the bar.

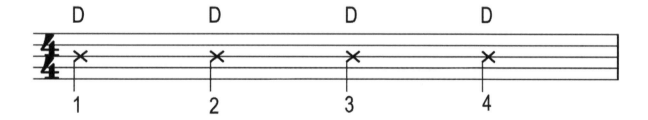

Remind yourself of this simple pattern by practicing it on some different chords of your choice.

Gone Sailing Song Sections

I've found that the best way to approach any new song is to break it up into sections and practice each one independently. Once you can play each section, you can join them up to play the entire song. Let's now apply this to *Gone Sailing*.

Exercise: Play the Intro

We'll use **strumming pattern 1** for the intro, performing 2 strums on Am and 1 strum on G and D.

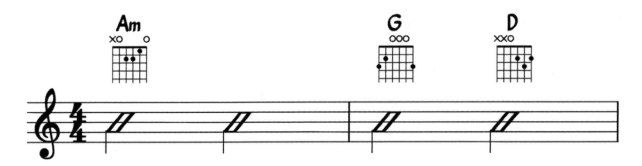

There are no repeat marks written, so we can assume the intro is only played once.

Practice playing the intro to *Gone Sailing* with the strumming I just described. Repeat it several times aiming for smooth changes and clean, ringing chords. Remember to look ahead for the next chord so that you're ready to change chords when it's time!

Pro Tip: as each song section becomes easier, practice playing it whilst looking at the *song sheet*, the way you'd keep your eyes on a piece of text you were reading. Being able to play *without* needing to look at your hands is easier than you might think, so make sure to work a bit of this into your practice sessions.

Exercise: Play the Verse

When playing the verse, use **strumming pattern 2**. This is shown in the following diagram:

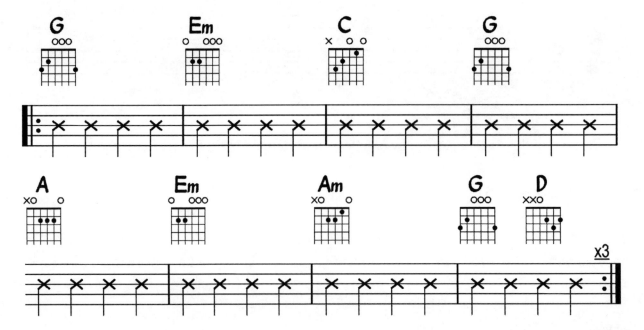

The verse is played 3 times in total (shown by the repeat marks and '**x3**').

Practice playing the verse with the strumming pattern. Begin by playing it just once. When you can do this, gradually add repetitions until you can smoothly play it 3 times without stopping.

Exercise: Add the Outro

The outro is exactly the same as the intro. Use the half note strumming pattern. This will help bring the song to a natural sounding close. After the D chord strum G to end the song.

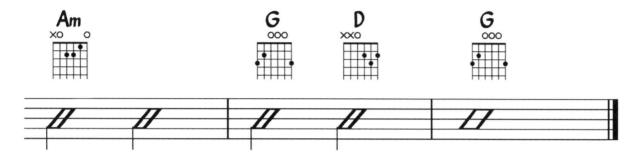

Practice playing the outro using the strumming shown.

Exercise: Gone Sailing, Full Performance

(See the **Gone Sailing Demo video** in the **Volume 1 videos** at **start-guitar.com** to help with this lesson).

Breaking a song up into sections is a great practice method, so don't be tempted to rush that step! Once you've done this and feel ready, join all the sections together and play *Gone Sailing* all the way through. The complete song is shown on the next song sheet, see how the strumming patterns have been added in this time.

A few tips before you get started:

- Use the different **strumming patterns** - it will sound more interesting and will help you keep your place in this repetitive song
- Keep **looking ahead** for the chord you're changing to!
- Don't forget the **repeat marks**, otherwise you'll end up in the wrong place

Try playing through the full song 4-5 times to get into the flow. A great way to practice the song is to play it along with the **demo video** I referenced a moment ago. Good luck!

Note: See the **free downloadable workbook** which comes with this book for a **printable** song sheet for *Gone Sailing*. Printing this and putting it on your music stand may be easier than trying to keep this book at the correct page! You can also practice playing *Gone Sailing* along with the **play-along backing track**. See the start of this book to find out how to download your workbook and the *Gone Sailing* backing track.

'Gone Sailing'

Performance Tips and Advice

Hopefully you feel like you're getting somewhere with the song! Next, we'll analyse your performance.

Which bits in the song are causing you difficulties? Perhaps a particular chord shape, chord change or strumming pattern is the problem? It's only by spotting our weaknesses and taking steps to fix them that we make any meaningful improvement, so isolate any problem areas and practice them intensively for 5-10 minutes using the methods we've employed so far in this book. Then, try the whole song again - has the problem area improved?

By tweaking and improving the elements of the song as you go, you'll start to notice it sounds better and better! Some things to think about are:

- Remember you're playing your first ever song here, and *everything* is new, so don't be surprised if it takes you a while to be able to play *Gone Sailing*. You might know the chords well, be comfortable with the chord pairs, and be confident with the strumming - but now you're doing all these things in the context of a *song*, and this feels quite different to practicing exercises
- *Get the song as good as you can for now*. Don't obsess about getting everything *perfect* or be overly self-critical when something goes wrong. Instead, focus on doing what needs to be done to improve. Operate in this way and mistakes and inconsistencies simply disappear over time
- Remember that your *next* song will be easier *because* you invested time in getting *Gone Sailing* as good as you could before you moved on - your playing will have greatly improved as a result!

That's all for Lesson 12: Ready To Move On?

Before you continue with this book series make sure that you:

- Can comfortably perform the chord pairs in *Gone Sailing* (with strumming)
- Can play each section of *Gone Sailing* (with chords and strumming)
- Can perform *Gone Sailing* all the way through (along with me in the video, on your own, and along with the play-along backing track)
- Feel ready for more!

When these points apply to you, you're ready to move on …

Congratulations: You've Reached the End of Chapter 3

You've achieved a lot in this chapter and can now:

- Change between commonly used pairs of chords, both with and without strumming
- Read and understand a basic song sheet
- Break a song up into chord pairs and sections and learn to play it (a method you can apply to *any* song you choose to learn!)
- Combine chord shapes, chord changing and strumming to play *Gone Sailing*

Check-off each of these goals in the **chapter 3 checklist** found in your free **workbook**. Doing this will help you see if you're definitely ready for more.

We have now covered many of the important approaches and practice methods used in this series. From this point on it's really just a case of applying these in different musical settings. So well done on making it this far, you've given yourself many of the tools you need to be successful on guitar!

As usual, I urge you to take your time working through the material in this chapter. Don't rush - enjoy the journey along the way - hopefully you're having a lot of fun with your guitar.

Good luck, and when you're ready we'll wrap up this book and talk about what's coming in Volume 2!

Final Words

Congratulations!

Awesome stuff ...you've reached the end of Volume 1 in the *Guitar for Beginners* series!

I hope you feel that this book has kickstarted you on your journey to becoming the guitar player you dream of becoming - if so, that's awesome.

Hopefully you're keen to continue learning with **Guitar for Beginners, Volume 2**, but before you do, I'd like to offer the following advice:

- Check you are 100% certain of the seven chord shapes we've been using so far - you'll be seeing them lots in the remainder of this book series
- Check you are 100% comfortable playing all the strumming patterns we've studied. This will give you a solid foundation on which to build your rhythm and strumming skills in future lessons
- Make sure you are familiar with the learning and practice methods we've used. We'll be using things like the throwing-away exercise, chord pairs and the chord circle in later lessons

Following these suggestions will prepare you for and help you get the most out of the remainder of this series. As I've said many times, don't be in too much of a rush; take your time, put in the work, and only move on when you genuinely feel like you're ready.

When you do feel like it's time to continue, I'll see you in book 2 where we'll:

- Complete your knowledge of the most essential guitar chords
- Expand your strumming skills with more patterns and exercises
- Boost your guitar skills and confidence by studying lots more songs!
- Study some more music theory basics

...and much more to help you become the guitarist you want to be!

Thanks for reading and learning with me, I hope it's been enjoyable and that you're delighted with the progress you've made since picking up this book.

Best of luck and I look forward to teaching you more in **Guitar for Beginners, Volume 2**!

James

Appendix 1: Learning Guitar Left Handed

As I said in the introduction, most guitar books teach from the viewpoint of a right-handed guitar player. This is understandable, but I want to make sure that both right *and* left-handed players can easily use these lessons. This appendix is designed to give the left-handed player what they need to successfully use this book. Let's look at the main things to consider when learning to play the guitar left-handed.

Considered Playing Right-Handed?

Even if you are naturally left-handed, I would *seriously* consider learning to play the guitar right-handed. I realise this may sound strange, but like it or not, there are definitely benefits to this approach.

Many world-class guitarists who are naturally left-handed play guitar as a right-hander, and if you begin this way you'll never know any difference anyway!

It's your decision to make, but don't assume that left-handed people *have* to play guitar left-handed, it's not the case.

Left Handed Guitars

In case you didn't know, playing left-handed requires a left-handed guitar!

Unfortunately, there is much less choice when it comes to left-handed guitars, but there are still lots of good options. Be prepared that you might sometimes have to pay a bit more too.

There are workarounds such as turning the guitar upside down or stringing it backwards - but the easiest option is probably just to get an instrument designed for the left-hander. I suggest you visit a good music store to find out more and try out some of the options.

Reverse the Hands!

- Right-handed guitarists strum with their right hand and fret the strings with their left hand. When playing left-handed this will be the **other way round**. In other words, you'll strum with your left hand and fret the strings with your right
- I've tried to use all-inclusive terms like *strumming hand* and *fretting hand* in this book, but other resources may not do the same. So, be prepared to reverse any instructions which refer to *right hand* or *left hand* - you'll likely need to 'flip' the hands round the other way if you're a left-handed guitarist

String Names, Frets and Finger Numbers Are the Same

Let's clarify some of the things covered in chapter 1 as they relate to the left-handed guitar player:

- Even though left handed guitars are strung 'back to front' when compared to right-handed instruments, the **string names** are the same. The thickest string is still the low E string, followed by the A, D, G, B and top E strings
- The **fingers on the fretting hand** are numbered 1-4 whether you play left or right handed
- The **frets** on the guitar are numbered in the same way whether you play left or right handed

Chord Boxes for the Left-Handed Player

Important: Before reading this make sure you understand the basics of how to read a chord diagram (see **Lesson 4**).

For the left-handed beginner guitarist one of the main challenges is that chord boxes may appear to be 'back-to-front'. Compare these two blank chord boxes and you'll see the strings are not in the same place on the diagrams. The **low E** (thickest string) is **highlighted** in both diagrams to make this difference easier to see:

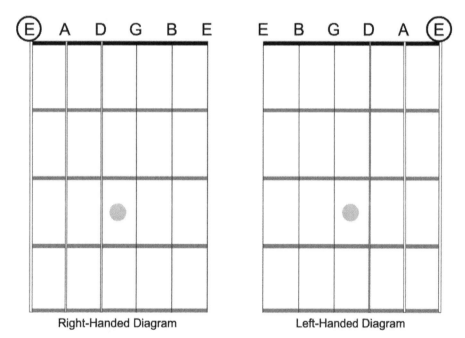

Right-Handed Diagram   Left-Handed Diagram

This means that the chord shapes themselves need to be written out differently. The left and right handed shapes will essentially be a mirror-image of each other.

For example, the G chord shape:

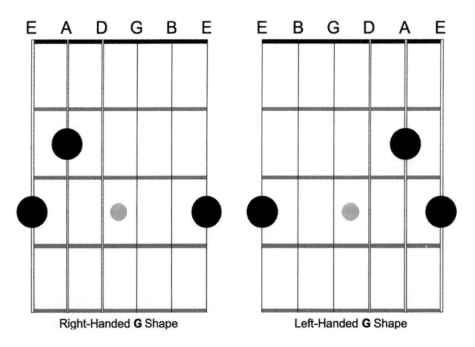

Right-Handed **G** Shape   Left-Handed **G** Shape

What does this mean for you as a left- handed guitar player?

For *many* left-handed players none of this makes any difference - they simply get used to using chord boxes written out for right-handed players and invert chord shapes as necessary. **This is something you eventually need to (and will) get comfortable doing**. This is important because most of the time chord diagrams will be written out for right-handed players and you need to be able to understand what they're showing you.

Having said that, this book is designed for the *beginner* guitarist, and I really don't want deciphering right-handed chord diagrams to become an obstacle for any left-handed guitar player!

For this reason I'm also including all the chord shapes covered in this book as **left-handed chord diagrams**. This will hopefully help anyone who feels like they need this extra resource when they're just getting started.

Left-Handed Chord Shapes

As stated earlier, you should aim to eventually be comfortable using right-handed chord boxes to learn chord shapes - this is important. In the meantime, these left-handed shapes may help you get started.

Remember:

- The 1st fret is numbered to help you locate where to play the chord shape
- The numbers marked on each note in the shape are fingering suggestions for your fretting hand - I recommend you follow these

Important: Remember that **all** the shapes in the main bulk of this book are shown right-handed. This includes any shapes shown in the exercises and songs I give you. To avoid mistakes, don't forget to use the following left-handed shapes instead (if you need to)!

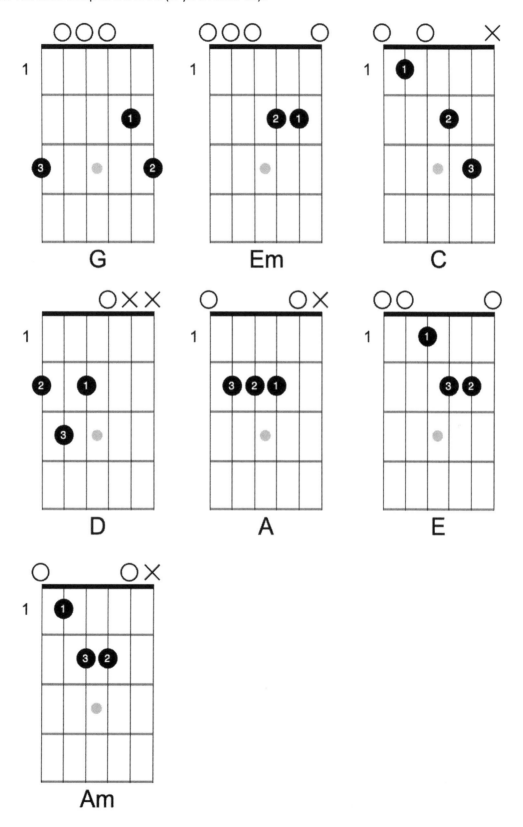

Guitar for Beginners, Volume 2

Continue your guitar playing journey with Volume 2 in the *Guitar for Beginners* method.

Build on what you've achieved so far and super-charge your beginner guitar skills with 12 easy-to-use guitar lessons showing you more of what you need to enjoy making music on the guitar.

In Volume 2 you'll:

- Build on your basic chord skills with more essential chord shapes and chord pairs (F, Dm, E7, A7 etc.)
- Learn more advanced strumming techniques and use them to play new and exciting strumming patterns
- Study and play 7 songs based on some of the most famous and popular songs of all time (video demos and play-along backing tracks provided!)
- Discover more exercises, speed-learning methods and practice routines to help you learn songs faster, memorise chords more easily, and continue to make speedy progress
- Learn useful playing tips, basic music theory, and much more to help you become the guitar player that you want to be!

Volume 2 includes bonus video lessons, exercises, and quizzes plus downloadable audio tracks and a printable workbook.

Available in paperback, hardback, spiralbound and ebook formats from Amazon.

More books by James Shipway

If you've enjoyed this book, you might like to check out some of my other titles, all available from Amazon or by request at your local bookshop:

Music Theory for Guitarists, the Complete Method Book, Volumes 1, 2 & 3 	**Music Theory for Guitarists, Volume 1** 	**Music Theory for Guitarists, Volume 2** 
The CAGED System for Guitar 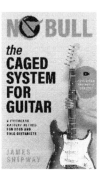	**Rock Lick Method for Guitar** 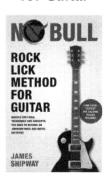	**Barre Chords for Guitar** 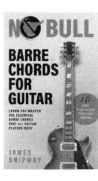
Circle of Fifths for Guitar 	**Blues Soloing for Guitar, Volume 1** 	**Blues Soloing for Guitar, Volume 2** 

Guitar for Beginners, Volume 1
by James Shipway

Published by Headstock Books
headstockbooks.com

Paperback ISBN: 978-1-914453-93-9
Hardcover ISBN: 978-1-914453-80-9 / 978-1-914453-81-6
Spiralbound ISBN: 978-1-914453-72-4
Ebook ISBN: 978-1-914453-94-6

Made in the USA
Monee, IL
03 February 2025

11434636R00048